PERFORMING TOUGH

Instrumentalist Version

Note: As an authorized purchaser of Performing Tough, you may download Dr. J. C. McCroskey's Relaxation audio in MP3 format from http://www.roberthstrickland.com/Relaxation/Relaxation.htm. (Case Sensitive) Click "Download the relaxation audio here." When prompted, type the User Name: "purchaser" and the Password: "authorized."

Powers and Strickland

PERFORMING TOUGH

By

Will Powers and Bob Strickland

Edited by: Lois Powers, Sue Strickland

Illustrated by: Bob and Sue Strickland

Published by:

Robert H Strickland Associates LLC

P. O. Box 1388

Everett, Washington 98206-1388 USA

Phone/Fax: 425-258-6796

All rights reserved. No part of this book may be reproduced or transmitted in any form or by any means, electronic or mechanical, including photocopying, recording, or by any information storage and retrieval system without written permission from the authors, except for the inclusion of brief quotations in a review.

Copyright 2016 by William G. Powers and Robert H. Strickland

Library of Congress Control Number: 2016941901

Powers, William G. 1943, and Strickland, Robert H., 1944

Performing Tough / by Will Powers and Bob Strickland

p. 98 cm.

Includes index.

ISBN 978-0-9635919-4-4

Dedication

Will and Lois Powers

"We dedicate our contribution to this book to our mothers (Mary T. Marquis and Frances M. Peterson). The foundation of our lives was strong and built upon the highest of values. We thank each parent for their strength and support during the entire course of our lives."

Bob and Sue Strickland

"We dedicate our contribution to the thousands of avid amateur and professional musicians who try to be as skilled as their time and physical capabilities allow. Also, we wish to recognize the efforts of the many professors and private instructors who spend countless hours pondering the mysteries of expressing oneself on an instrument for no reasons other than to help himself, herself, and others play just a little bit better.

Among these, Bob includes those who gave hims a keen appreciation of music, such as Bob's mother, Erna Strickland, his friend, high school orchestra conductor, Otto Michaels, his trumpet teachers, Joe Cinquemani and Clint McLaughlin, and the many fine musicians that he has shared the stage with in over 40 years.

Sue's inspirations include her husband Bob, her fellow musicians during a formative nine years of classical violin training, and her instructors in music and graphic arts. Sue has a profound appreciation for the art of jazz and performing arts, admiring greatly the artists' dedication to effective practice and their drive to achieve illuminating performances."

Acknowledgements

This book has been a family project from the very beginning. Each of us acknowledge the support, sensitive editing, and integration of specialized knowledge from each of the four contributors (Will/Lois and Bob/Sue). Without each other, this project would never have been completed.

From Will Powers: Special thanks go to Bruce McDonald, Dr. James C. McCroskey and Dr. H. Wayland Cummings for delivering appropriate "motivational stimulation" at various points in my life development which ultimately led to my ability to contribute to this project.

From Bob Strickland: Thanks go to my long-time friends, Carter Stanfield, trombonist with the Macon Georgia Symphony and Rob Jonas, lead trumpeter extroidinaire in our band, Swingtime 2000, for helping me enjoy experiences in music that, for years, I believed was not to come my way.

The authors acknowledge the following organizations for providing some of the images used in this book:

"Presentation Task Force" - New Vision Technologies, Incorporated, 38 Auriga Drive, Unit 13, Nepean, Ontario Canada, K2E 8A5, Telephone: 613-727-8184. Copyrighted, All Rights Reserved.

Pixabay
Braxmeier & Steinberger GbR (VAT Reg.No.: DE297456622),
Hans Braxmeier, Donaustraße 13, 89231 Neu-Ulm, Germany
Phone: +49 (0)731 / 800 1660
info(at)pixabay.com (https://pixabay.com/)

Forward

Every performance is filled with potential high-pressure or clutch situations. Players who perform well in the clutch, Perform Tough.

Players who perform well under pressure are admired because this ability is rare. They "stay in there", playing as close to the ideal as they can. They are "locked in" mentally, all of the time.

People who fail to play well under pressure simply don't know how to establish a successful Performing Tough mentality.

To be successful under pressure, you need to know:
- How you — yourself — create your own clutch situations.
- What happens to your body in clutch situations.
- Methods to ensure high-quality performance under pressure.
- How to make these methods automatic through practice.
- How to use these methods in all forms of playing.

We want you to be a success by learning how to:
- Make personal "success decisions."
- Relax under pressure.
- Increase your self-confidence.
- Practice success on and off of the stage.
- Make a "mental routine" work for you.

Performing Tough shows you how to use a few simple, proven mental skills to put you in control of what you want to accomplish. If you use these methods faithfully, you will eagerly take on responsibility for your own performance. You will be a master of your own success.

These methods will make you a problem-solver. You will stop blaming yourself, your equipment, external conditions, or even other persons for your failures. You will understand that no one is successful all of the time. Failure will become just another opportunity to seek solutions and play better the next time.

Even if you master only one method and use it consistently, you should see a dramatic increase in your performance potential under conditions that are extremely stressful for others. At the very least, you will get greater enjoyment and less frustration from music.

Use the encouraging "Keys" throughout this book to help you remember what to do. Let's begin now, so you can start using these mental skills with your own physical skills right away! Here is your first key.

 **Work hard, be persistent, learn the strategies, and review the keys often. Success in performance will become much easier for you. You will Perform Tough!**

Like everything else that is worthwhile and rare, Performing Tough does not come without belief, change, dedication, and practice. The only real question you must answer is "Do I really want to improve my playing performance?" If you answer "Yes!", it's just a question of "want to" and "know how to!"

Disclaimer

The techniques described herein, like those recommended by others, may not be effective for all persons. Therefore, the authors/publisher disclaim any responsibility and liability in connection with any actions taken or not taken based on the content of this book.

Will Powers, Ph. D., Lewisville, Texas

Bob Strickland, M. S., Everett, Washington

Contents

Dedication 5

Acknowledgements 7

Forward 9
    Disclaimer 10

1   You Can Perform Tough! 13
    Clutch Situations 13
    How Does a Clutch Situation Develop? 15
    The Ultimate Clutch Solution: Your Mind 21
    Mental Control and the Physical Skills 22

2   You Can Consciously Choose to Be a Success! 25
    Non-conscious Decision # 1: To Get Anxious or Stressed out 26
    Non-conscious Decision # 2: To Fear Failure 27
    Non-conscious Decision # 3: To Fear Success 28
    Non-conscious Decision # 4: To Believe That You Will Fail 29
    Non-conscious Decision # 5: To Believe That It Just Doesn't Matter ... 30
    Non-conscious Decision # 6: To Tense Up and Try Harder 31
    Non-conscious Decision # 7: To Become Distracted 32
    Non-conscious Decision # 8: To Practice Only the Physical Skills 33
    Conscious Decisions: The Hidden Success Options 34

3   You Can Build Self-confidence! 37
    Taking Control of Yourself 37
    Self-talk and Behavior Drills 41

4   You Can Use the Super Powers of Your Mind! 49
    Visualizing Your Way to Success 49
    Mental Practice Drills 54

5	You Can Relax, Anywhere, Anytime!.. 63	
	Using Willful Relaxation 63	
	Relaxation Drills 68	
6	You Can Make Mental Toughness Routine! 73	
	Taking Control of Your Mental Environment 73	
	Mental Toughness Routine 74	
	MTR Incorporation Drill 77	
	A Final Word..78	

Appendix A Building Reliable Physical Skills 81
    Popular Music Performance Books 81

Appendix B Making a Relaxation Tape or CD 85
    Making a Relaxation Tape or CD..85

Appendix C Making a Coping and Booster Tape or CD............................. 89
    Making a Coping Tape or CD 89
    Making a Booster (Relaxation with Coping) Tape or CD 92

1 You Can Perform Tough!

Performing Tough is successfully meeting the mental challenge of performing well, regardless of the difficulty of the music or the amount of pressure a player is experiencing. It is easiest to see if someone is Performing Tough when the pressure level is high, often called a "clutch" situation. **Clutch situations are common in music because players come under pressure fairly often.**

Clutch Situations

People "in the clutch" definitely place themselves under pressure, stress, and tension simply because they have an extremely high desire to succeed. **A clutch situation develops when someone experiences an unusually strong emotional reaction related to achieving one or more important goals (like nailing an audition or playing a complicated piece of music with no mistakes).**

You Can Perform Tough!

We never forget those special moments in music when we desire success more than anything else. Almost every player, regardless of his or her particular instrument, can tell you about one instance in which he or she has met the challenge of performing well in a clutch situation — Performing Tough. Those times when we have achieved our goals stand out in our minds, especially if such successes are few and far between.

Of course, most of us also vividly remember those instances when we did not perform well under pressure. Although we put those negative memories in the backs of our minds, they are still there and active. These negatives create a very clear history the next time we are in a similar situation. Then, the history in our minds tends to repeat itself.

Because we focus so much upon the potential for failure, we do not perform well in the clutch. **Unfortunately, we often create unreasonable expectations of ourselves.** We think we should be perfect and succeed all of the time. And when we do not meet these expectations, we tend to feel that we are failures.

 Take a really good look at what you expect from yourself and then ask, "Are my expectations reasonable?"

After all is said and done, few professional players ever perform at their true potential in clutch situations. The ones who do, cannot do it 100% of the time. You can see this for yourself during any given performance, either live on television. **If elite professionals have difficulty executing in the clutch, is it reasonable for you to expect a superior level of performance from yourself — all of the time? Probably not!** In fact, if at your best you succeed 90% of the time, then under high-pressure playing conditions, your most reasonable expectation would be that you will succeed 90% of the time. If a particular instance happens to be one of the 90%, then that is super! If it happens to be one of the 10%, then that is too bad. **Be reasonable with yourself; dwelling on "failure" because of unreasonable expectations is absolutely foolish!**

If you have reasonable expectations, you still may not perform as well in the clutch as you would like, simply due to a lack of know-how and practice. But, you can perform up to your potential if you put as much hard work into your mental skills as you do into your physical skills. The mental skills are actually quite simple — just common sense.

Every player practices the physical skills of how to play his or her instrument. Few actually practice their mental skills other than the cognitive (conscious) ones of understanding the music to be played. But consistent achievers have their mental acts together. They practice and use mental skills consistently even though they may not be aware that these skills are being used. Therefore, they perform well under pressure!

The consistent and effective mental control of refined physical skills distinguishes real long-term achievers from the rest of the field.

 **You can practice mental and physical skills at the same time!**

We show you how you can practice physical and mental skills at the same time. Learn and practice the methods of mental control and put them into your plan – all of the time. You will have more frequent success under pressure.

How Does a Clutch Situation Develop?

At any time in any kind of highly competitive environment, you can become involved in a clutch situation. The word "clutch" is more commonly associated with sports, while the words "stage fright" or "musical performance anxiety (MPA)" have become associaed with music.

In the academic world, much study has been devoted to understanding MPA, defined as *the experience of persisting, distressful apprehension about and/or actual impairment of, performance skills in a public context, to a degree unwarranted given the individual's musical aptitude, training, and level of preparation.* **In essence, all of these terms attempt to describe what happens when you experience an unusually strong emotional reaction related to achieving one or more important goals.**

> **Note:** It is somewhat inaccurate that the distress associated with live performances is often attributed by clinicians and teachers to "insufficient performance experience", "faulty technique", "inappropriate repertoire", or "improper practice and preparation habits." As pointed out by Dr. Paul G. Salmon, "Performance anxiety, (AKA "clutch situations") afflicts many veteran performers with exemplary skills and preparatory techniques as well, and such eminent musicians as Artur Rubenstein, Pablo Casals, and Luciano Pavarotti have all reported experiencing extreme tension and psychological distress while performing before audiences."

For example, you may begin playing a composition with very little pressure on you. But, as the piece of music progresses and the score becomes more intense, the pressure may reach such a high level that a clutch situation develops for you. **The player who "performs tough" will maintain control longer and more frequently.**

Some examples of potential clutch situations are:
- Needing to prepare for a performance
- Needing to master difficult passages
- Needing to memorize several complicated lines
- Needing to navigate several key changes
- Needing to maintain a system of transposition
- Needing to recover immediately after making a mistake
- Needing to overcome a physical ailment to perform adequately

Clutch situations are very personal. A clutch situation to one person may not produce stress or tension in another. You make your own!

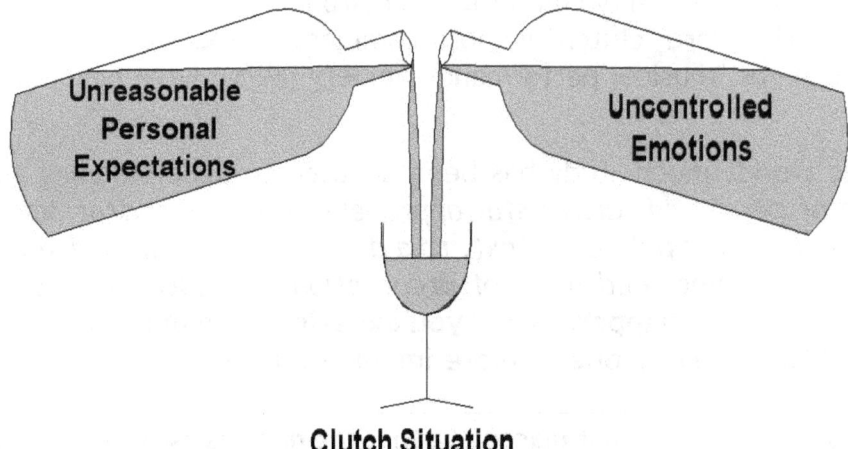

Clutch Situation

Each person makes his/her own personal clutch situations! This is a result of two basic problems:
- Unreasonable personal expectations
- Uncontrolled emotions

We call these "clutch problems", and we would like you to understand them. Keep in mind that every performer experiences one or more of these problems at some time in his or her development, but those who Perform Tough under pressure have learned to solve these problems.

Clutch Problem #1: Trying To Achieve Unreasonable Goals

A goal is a specific idea of what you wish to achieve — an expectation. Success to most performers involves the achievement of three goals:

- The Execution — the quality of sound, attack, dynamics, interpretation, etc.
- The Performance — the overall quality of the performance
- The Reward — satisfaction, recognition, or monitary gain.

These are shown in the diagram below.

1. **The first level goal, execution with the peak accuracy needed to play a passage perfectly is the only goal that is under your direct control.** It is the foundation achievement that actually allows you an opportunity to reach the second level, or intermediate, goal. Execution is the important goal. The frequency of trouble-free performance (the outcome) will rise naturally as quality of execution improves.

2. **The second level goal, the overall high-quality performance outcome, is not under your direct control.** You may get a bad break, such as a malfunctioning microphone, a broken string, or an intonation problem among fellow players, even during a well-executed passage, for example. Remember, "Good players do not play notes! They play music!"

3. **The third level goal, the reward of satisfaction, recognition, or money is never under your control.** Anything that is not under your direct control should not even

enter your mind. You should ignore it at all times, or you will allow it to interfere with your performance.

Focus on the goal that is within your immediate reaching distance. Do not focus upon goals that are not under your direct control.

Having lofty ambitions is wonderful! There is absolutely nothing wrong with your dreaming of being the professional best, for example. But, if you focus upon that high-level goal instead of the most immediate and reachable goal of a perfectly-executed passage, you may never reach the higher one. You can maintain consistent success results and reach great heights if you place easier goals as "stepping stones" in front of you on the way to more difficult ones.

> **Example:** You must execute well (Goal 1) before you can perform well (Goal 2). You must perform well before you can reap the reward of a superior performance (Goal 3). You cannot bypass Goal 1! But, if you achieve Goal 1, you will achieve Goal 2, and possibly, Goal 3.

If you allow even a small bit of your focus on Goal 1 (execution) to drift to Goal 2 (performing) or Goal 3 (reward), you lower your potential to execute. You corrupt your ability to make the physical movements that allow good execution and excellence of performance!

The first major contribution to your performance success in clutch situations is to focus only upon that immediate goal under your direct control. Place your complete mental concentration only on the goal of perfect execution, one note at a time!

Clutch Problem #2: Letting Your Emotions Get Out Of Control.

Emotions are often troublesome when trying to perform in high-stress situations. Negative emotions destroy positive potential.

Think about the times when you practiced your instrument while angry. You would tense up and make mistakes in places that you had previously mastered. When you were depressed, you would give up and make a sound without any attention to its quality. This illustrates that you cannot practice productively when you are upset or emotional.

On the other hand, positive emotions promote positive potential. When you experience positive emotions, you carefully choose an isolated and relaxed setting for practice. You use practice to develop and refine muscle habits associated with a high-quality execution and sound. Some of your finest playing is done during practice under conditions of positive emotion. You repeat effective movements over and over in a relaxed condition; you concentrate!

The second major contribution to your performance success in clutch situations is to create the same mental environment in both performance and practice. Create the same emotions during performance that you create during practice.

A few players can do this by making practice like performance. But for most players, the key to their success is making performance more like practice. This definitely does not mean that practice is play time and performance becomes just a time to play. **It means that the mental approach you use in practice should be the same one you use during performance.**

The Ultimate Clutch Problem: What Happens to Your Body in a Clutch Situation?

What is the major emotional difference between a practice environment and a competitive environment? It is the presence of a prize for performing well or a penalty for performing poorly! During performance, your desire to achieve important goals (good execution or winning) combines with your fear of possible failure, causing negative emotions to rise within you. Clutch situations impact your body's ability to perform at a consistently high level.

In the heat of performance with a significant outcome, most players will eventually focus on the outcome, allowing their attention to stray from the all-important performance. This is exactly why so many players are not great performers! If you fall into this trap, you become emotionally and physically stressed. You become "emotional." Your muscles become tense and your movements erratic. You lose the fine physical edge you developed during practice. Realizing that you have lost the "feel" of reliable movements, you become even more emotional, and your performance suffers even more.

We humans are strange critters. When our minds are relaxed, our bodies are relaxed. When our minds are up-tight, our bodies get up-tight. **An unemotional robot is an excellent mental model. But, because humans can never hope to achieve a robot's lack of emotion, we have to do what is necessary to wipe out the negative emotions that interfere with our performance under stressful conditions.**

You can have emotional control! Just begin a systematic plan for developing, practicing, and using mental skills during practice and performance.

> **Example:** Assume that you really, really want to play well so your band or orchestra can win a competition. However, you know that you haven't been playing well lately and fear that you will not perform well now.

These negative thoughts and emotions interfere with the ability of your muscles to execute at the relaxed level you achieve during practice. The anticipation of failing to reach the second level goal (high-quality performance) causes nervousness (anxiety) that keeps your muscles from executing the movements with peak accuracy and consistency.

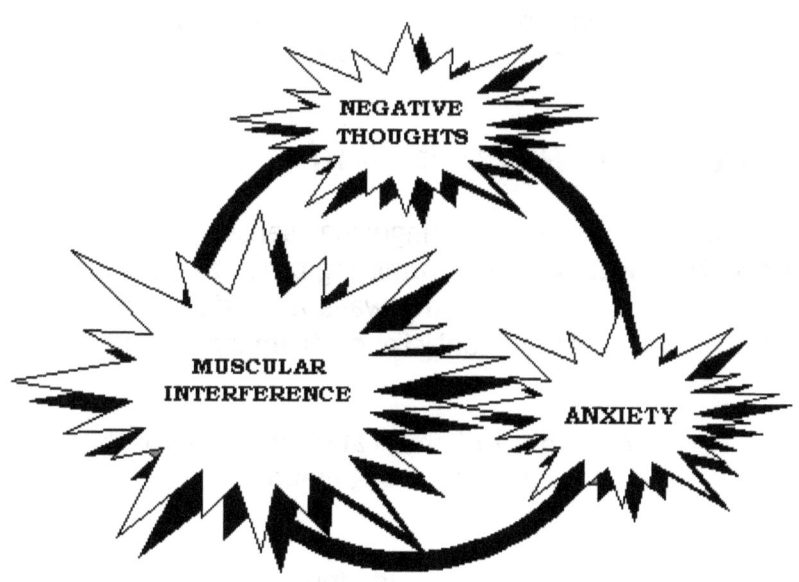

Anxiety and a smooth performance cannot go hand-in-hand. Anxiety represents an obstacle that we must overcome to reach our goals successfully.

The Ultimate Clutch Solution: Your Mind

Your thoughts are your reality — regardless of what is actually happening. Therefore, any situation that you believe is "clutch" is indeed clutch — to you.

Your thoughts about your situation, your ability to perform, and the importance of your goals produce the framework within which your body has to make accurate and consistent movements. The situation is alive; you cannot be neutral. You always react in some way to the situation. Your key to success is to get your mind working for you — not against you.

 **You can willfully change how you think and act.**

Those situations that are "bad" can become "not so bad" after all. You have a miraculous ability to bring about change. Just make a choice to think and act differently. Your success or failure is under your control through what you choose to believe; it is truly up to you! As you become more successful in clutch situations, your confidence will grow, opening the door to future success.

Later, we show you how to restructure your thoughts to produce a reasonable reality, allowing you to perform at your maximum talent level. However, at this point, it is important to consider some points about the physical skills of music.

Mental Control and the Physical Skills

If you have poor physical skills (air flow, fingering, sense of pitch, rhythm, or style) you must improve them so they will not be a stumbling block to your progress in using mental skills. While it is true that there are many ways a musician can play, some habits are structurally unsound and do not allow consistency or improvement.

 **Consistency of physical skills is vital to the development of strong mental skills.**

You must be able to trust your senses and your movements to produce the same correct results every time. Otherwise, it will be impossible to build confidence, no matter how well you apply the mental skills explained in this book! If you have sound, consistent physical skills, mental skills are of tremendous benefit to you! To help you with your physical skills, we offer the following guidelines.

1. **Make sure that your mouthpieces are of a correct fit to allow you good control on each and every note.** You may not be aware of unproductive movements, but they will prevent you from developing the proper mental focus and building confidence.

2. **Make sure that your instrument is of sufficient quality to play notes cleanly, on pitch, and with predictable air support.** Keep the instrument clean and in good working condition.

3. **Establish an ongoing relationship with an instructor or coach who understands the physical skills, who is a skilled observer, listener, and teacher, and who will help you attain your goals.**

4. **Make sure that each and every attack is decisive and the notes stable.** If you cannot think of a reason to strike and hold a note in a certain way, eliminate it!

5. **Develop your physical skills around the logical.** Think through everything you hear, discussing it with your instructor, ensuring that you understand why you make your own collection of movements and behaviors. Everything you do must have a valid reason. See **Appendix A Building Reliable Physical Skills** for a list of excellent instrumental instructional books and references.

The following chapters describe three different ways to improve your potential to perform well under stressful conditions. One or more of these methods will work for you. You may find that all three methods will work together to give you the best results, performing as well as you are physically capable of under pressure.

 **You are in control! Consciously choose what you want to focus your thoughts on. Performing Tough is simple and easy. It takes a bit of practice but once you've mastered the basics, Performing Tough becomes second nature.**

2 You Can Consciously Choose to Be a Success!

We frequently do not think about how we will react in many situations, even when our reactions may be important to our personal success potential! Rather, we develop non-conscious habits, reacting to whatever happens without thinking about it. These habits control our lives; for example, do you still think about how to tie your shoes?

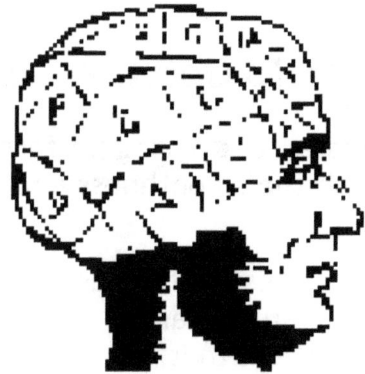

Because we react without thinking about the circumstances, many of our decisions are non-conscious. With non-conscious decisions, the potential to make errors — to react inappropriately in any given situation — is very high. There are many such non-conscious decisions that produce error and increase the potential for failure.

 Non-conscious decisions are always poor decisions. They are like letting your worst enemy make your decisions for you!

In this chapter, we explain many non-conscious decisions that keep players from performing at their full potential. Potentially good players who do poorly in performance have made one or more of the following non-conscious decisions for themselves!

- To get anxious or stressed out
- To fear failure
- To fear success
- To believe that they will fail
- To believe that it just doesn't matter
- To tense up and try harder
- To become distracted
- To practice only the physical music

To avoid the destructive effect that such non-conscious decisions have on your skills, you need to understand what these decisions mean and what tough performers do to overcome them. Let's look at them one-by-one.

Non-conscious Decision # 1: To Get Anxious or Stressed out

If you are mentally anxious or stressed out during performance, you will be physically up-tight and unable to execute with the smoothness and consistency that you have in practice.

Tough performers are not immune to stress. They just deal with it effectively. Because they know that anxiety or stress is a natural part of high-level performance, they simply meet it head-on and control their reactions to it.

They have a plan that involves using exactly the methods explained in this book. They use mental skills to overcome stress.

 Meet stress head-on and take control!

Non-conscious Decision # 2: To Fear Failure

Some people fear failure, but no one can reasonably expect to be successful all of the time. It's that simple. A major difference between people who perform well in the clutch and those who don't is how reasonable their self-expectations are.

Tough performers know that they play very well — 90% of the time, for example. They may also know that if they execute well, they will reach the secondary goal of a good performance. Of course, some of the time they will fail because of something beyond their control, such as sticky valves, a broken string, a malfunctioning stand light, a high wind blowing the music away, etc.

Because tough performers know their odds, they do not fear failure. They are more reasonable about the demands they make on themselves. They concentrate on achieving only that which is in their control — high-quality execution. If they happen to experience one of the 10 poor instances out of 100 that do not have a good result, it's unfortunate but not devastating. They know that they can reasonably expect to be successful 90 times out of 100.

 **Mentally, the tough performers focus on the rate of success — not the rate of failure. They know that over the long haul, the odds are with them, not against them.**

Non-conscious Decision # 3: To Fear Success

Although difficult to believe, some people actually decide to fear being successful! They think that if they become too successful then everyone will expect success from them all of the time. Because they know that they cannot be successful all of the time, it presents an assured failure situation.

So, in a backwards sort of way, the fear of ultimate failure produces a fear of immediate success that produces the anxiety that guarantees the body will not perform well in clutch situations. As this long, complicated reasoning occurs, it obviously creates an environment of failure.

Tough performers know that no one expects them to be successful all of the time. They do not expect the same of themselves either! They know that, if they set their sights on goals that they can achieve, bigger successes will follow. They do not fear success because they are successful in reaching realistic goals all of the time.

 **Tough performers do not expect to be successful all of the time.**

Non-conscious Decision # 4: To Believe That You Will Fail

Some players remain "hung up" on the times that they have failed (the 10% factor). As they find themselves in a clutch situation, they remind themselves that, because they haven't performed well in the past, they will not perform well in the present situation. Remember how the body believes the mind? If you believe you are going to fail, the odds are the body will make every effort for these thoughts to come true.

Tough performers are aware of the times when they failed — but only for a short time. They simply "go back to the drawing board" and work out a winning strategy.

Failure drops from their minds as they work productively on their physical and mental skills in anticipation of the next performance.

 **Tough performers go back to the drawing board.
Failure drops from their minds.**

You Can Consciously Choose to Be a Success!

Non-conscious Decision # 5: To Believe That It Just Doesn't Matter

Once again, the mind dictates to the body. **If you convince yourself that it doesn't really matter whether you execute well, the body believes you and doesn't bother to execute well.** It becomes a self-fulfilling prophecy.

Tough performers get a good feeling from a well-executed passage. To them, the proper feel and anticipation of a well-played piece of music is often more confidence-boosting than the playing itself. They are performance-oriented. They "get a kick" out of a well played passage — both in practice and in performance. To them, every note matters!

 Tough performers get a kick out of a well-executed passage.

Non-conscious Decision # 6: To Tense Up and Try Harder

In sports such as football or boxing, success depends upon explosive force and tremendous exertion of muscle. Playing an instrument is very different. Success is dependent upon smooth execution created by the proper balance between relaxation and tension. As soon as you try to "give it everything you've got," your muscular balance goes out of whack — and so does your ability to execute well.

It is easy to spot a player who tenses up under pressure. A tense player may think that "trying harder" involves stiffening up and compressing the torso (thereby interfering with breathing), wearing a stern, concerned expression, making edgy movements, and rushing the tempo beyond what the composer intended.

If the player is particularly "keyed up", he may follow one mistake with another and an even edgier series of movements. **An up-tight player may even fly off the handle.**

Tough performers are also tempted to physically overpower a stressful situation! But they do not give in to temptation. They systematically take their playing positions, calm their minds and bodies, focus, and play in an unhurried, high-quality fashion. This is Performing Tough under pressure.

 **Tough performers systematically calm themselves, focus, and confidently play.**

You Can Consciously Choose to Be a Success!

Non-conscious Decision # 7: To Become Distracted

When you are distracted, it means that you have made an unconscious decision not to concentrate. Playing requires complete concentration and internal focus. When your mind is busy looking outside of execution factors, it is not sufficiently focused.

A lack of concentration on the immediate task of a high-quality execution opens the door to "seeing" extraneous movement or "hearing" noises that are typically easy to "shut out", but which are now allowed to become disruptive.

Tough performers are so focused that they would not even notice "fans" screaming, yelling, and waving their arms in the audience. Proper mental focus is a simple decision to make — not a hard one. Just like the physical skills, the mental skills take practice to achieve.

 Tough performers concentrate and stay focused, no matter what is going on around them.

Non-conscious Decision # 8: To Practice Only the Physical Skills

Many players feel that all they have to do to improve clutch performance is practice the physical skills more and practice more intensely. This is not practicing smart!

Don't get us wrong. Practicing the physical skills is important for developing and refining playing techniques. If you have mechanically poor movements or air support, you cannot control your technique physically or mentally! **But merely practicing notes, passages, or memorizing long compositions more or harder will do absolutely nothing for the mental skills that become critical for success under clutch conditions.**

To perform at maximum physical potential in clutch situations you have to learn the rules of the mind and practice, practice, practice the mental skills.

Practice the Mental Skills as You Would the Physical Skills

Tough performers practice their mental skills right along with their physical skills. Much of their playing is done during performance, therefore, they use mental skills more frequently than recreational players. But, the point is that they know mental skills and use them all of the time. They do not play without a purpose. They do not mindlessly strike notes. They use their minds to create consistently good sounds.

Your battle plan for success involves forcing negative, non-conscious decisions up to the conscious level. Then, make positive conscious decisions about your reactions to situations. These decisions determine your success or failure potential and deserve your best, thoughtful efforts; they involve you!

Unless you consciously recognize your negative non-conscious decisions and change them, they will usually stay in your non-conscious level of awareness. Just like a law, they will stay in force! They will continue to interfere with your performance and lower your confidence.

You Can Consciously Choose to Be a Success!

Conscious Decisions: The Hidden Success Options

Your approach to consistent high-quality execution under stress begins with consciously selecting the following options that work best for you! All of the options covered in this book work; the question you must answer is, **"Which options work best to make me comfortable in the situations where I need help?"**

Therefore, here is a list of the following chapters that describe the basic success options in detail; you should choose from these. "Seriously try" each and every one of the options exactly in the manner we describe. Then, follow the lead of many players and incorporate into your performance system all of the options that make sense to you, that fit your personality, and allow you to reach your goals.

You will be able to achieve the goals listed under each chapter heading, below.

Chapter 3 You Can Build Self-confidence!
- Increase your confidence through what you say to yourself and others.
- Establish the correct frame of mind for success.
- Act like a success.

Chapter 4 You Can Use the Super Powers of Your Mind!
- Visualize successful execution.
- Practice mental skills anytime, anywhere.
- Focus your mind for consistent, successful performance.

Chapter 5 You Can Relax, Anywhere, Anytime!
- Relax physically and mentally.
- Set and achieve realistic goals for yourself.
- Increase your knowledge of yourself and how you really feel about and react to real situations.

Chapter 6 You Can Make Mental Toughness Routine!
- Organize your thoughts and actions for consistent, high-level performance in practice and in performance.

It is easy and simple to perform well under both regular and special conditions. All it takes is useful knowledge and practice, practice, practice!

 You can have a calmer, more systematic approach to music especially during performance. You can Perform Tough; and others will marvel at your skill in the clutch, never even realizing what you are doing.

You Can Consciously Choose to Be a Success!

3 You Can Build Self-confidence!

The relationship between the mind and body is amazing. Your body simply cannot tell the difference between reality and your imagination. **What the mind tells the body to believe, the body believes.**

> **Example: Do you know of anyone who had a nightmare and woke up sweating, screaming and flailing about? Even though the nightmare was only imagined, the mind convinced the body it was actually happening, and the body reacted.**

Taking Control of Yourself

The following sections describe the concepts of thoughts, conversation, and behavior. See the **Self-talk and Behavior Drills** section for detailed directions.

Thoughts (Self-talk)

Thoughts are a form of programming, or "talking to" your brain. The key to success or failure in music is programming the mind. If you program your mind to tell the body it will fail, then the body will fail. **However, if you program the mind to tell the body it will succeed, then the body will succeed.** The secret to all of this is that the mind has to believe the scenario you present. If the mind believes, the body believes. Thinking positive gives your muscles the best chance for a high-quality execution.

 Destructive Self-talk Off — Productive Self-talk On!

The extent to which your mind believes you will be successful is directly related to what you tell it to believe. So, you have to start by exploring what you tell yourself about yourself. If this self-talk is not productive, then all you have to do is replace destructive thoughts with productive self-talk. It's easy!

Talking With Others

Another form of programming your brain is the actual talk you have with others about your potential to succeed. So often, we hear many players predicting failure for themselves. "No way can I play this part correctly!", or "I am not very good at trills and runs." Most of the time, they are good fortune tellers because their brains hear this talk and believe that it should produce a failure event.

 **Say positive things; do not say negative things!**

The real trick is to say positive things to get the odds in your favor. Some positive statements are, "I will play the next eight measures flawlessly.", or "I will strike each note thoughtfully." Obviously, simply talking positively will not automatically produce success for you every time. But, getting the odds in your favor will have an undeniable impact on your execution.

Behavior

Any action you take that disrupts a positive mental attitude puts the odds against your success. When frustrated, some players commonly engage in disruptive behavior, such as:

- Throwing the music on the floor
- Cursing
- Kicking the floor
- Stomping around other players in the area
- Purposely acting disgusted

All of these actions detract from the positive mental focus needed for high-quality execution during the next passage.

Contrary to what many people think, being a jerk does not "release" your frustrations and allow you to concentrate on your next passages. Instead, such behaviors form part of your mental history and serve as a reality check for the brain. In other words, these types of behaviors confirm that you are expecting failure. With all of this mental energy focused on failure, it is not surprising that successful execution in the clutch is a rare event.

The most productive action you can take involves knowing the difference between what is in your control and what is not in your control. A flawless performance is simply not a sure thing. It is not constantly under your control.

 Frustration over conditions not under your control is a total waste of mental energy. Focus only on that which is under your control – high-quality execution.

Recognizing Negatives

Negative thoughts, talk, and behavior often originate from a non-conscious level. Therefore, they can be very difficult to recognize. **Yet, if you cannot identify what you are thinking, saying, and doing, you cannot correct the situation and improve your success potential.**

 Self-awareness is the first step to progress! Listen to yourself.

Replacing Negatives with Positives

Once you know how to recognize negatives, what should you do about them? The answer is to replace them with positives!

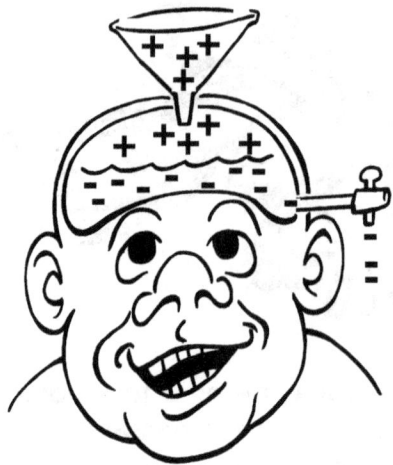

Do not emphasize "getting rid" of bad habits. To do so may result in keeping them. Rather, emphasize substituting good habits for bad ones. This is a more productive and successful approach.

 Substitute good, positive habits for bad, negative ones.

Practicing Positive Thinking, Talking, and Behaving

Once you know positive things to think, to say, and to do, it is your responsibility to enact them at all times. Even though you may be enthusiastic at first, it still may be a little difficult to catch yourself applying negatives. However, you may be able to get a little help from your playing partners. Tell them what you are trying to accomplish. Be honest! Ask them to let you know every time you slip up and move toward negative talk or behavior. Make it fun for them to tell you or they won't help you. Volunteer to contribute to your playing partners every time they catch you.

In a very short time, you will be able to change your perspective and enhance your ability to perform effectively under the worst conditions. This joint helping project will also contribute to cohesiveness and spirit.

 **Be a success by thinking like a success, talking like a success, and acting like a success.**

Self-talk and Behavior Drills

For the drills on the following pages, keep a notebook so you can see your total progress. Label a page or section with the name of the drill at the top. Your notes are private, so keep them to yourself.

Recognizing Negatives

This drill is designed to help you recognize negative thoughts, talk, and behavior that you may not be aware of. Follow the directions below; think hard, and be honest with yourself! Self-awareness is the first step toward progress!

Directions

In the space below, write a list of negative thoughts, talk, and behavior that you remember doing. Make these items specific and list as many as you want; use your notebook or a separate sheet of paper if necessary. Then, show the list to friends and ask them to add anything they have noticed that is not on your list.

> **Example:** "I stomp the floor whenever I am angry." or "When I do not play well the first time through, I loaf during the second attempt." or "I curse when I miss a note."

a. _____

b. _____

c. _____

d. _____

e. _____

Replacing Negatives with Positives

This drill is an extension of the previous one. **Once you know what your negative thoughts, talk, and behavior are, you need to replace them with positives.** If you do not replace them, other negatives will take the place of the ones that you have abandoned. Nature hates a void! It is better to decide for yourself what to replace abandoned negatives with. Follow the directions below; think hard, and be honest with yourself!

Directions

Now, write a list of positive thoughts, talk and behavior that you would like to replace those on the "neagtives" list. Be specific. Be reasonable.

> **Example:** "When I am angry, I take a deep breath and relax.", or "When I make a mistake, I welcome the opportunity to play it again as a chance to practice."

a.

b.

c.

d.

e.

Practicing Self-talk at Home or When Alone

Take control of your thoughts. Use your "quiet time" to eliminate negative self-statements by replacing them with positive, reasonable statements about yourself. Examine your own self-talk by "thinking out loud", talking rather than merely thinking the thoughts. You will be surprised to learn how much you put yourself down when it is completely undeserved.

1. Draw up a chart as shown under **Recording Results**.
2. Take at least 15 minutes each day in private to evaluate yourself — your intelligence, your skill, your talent, your physical appearance. Talk to yourself out loud, noting what you say is positive or negative.
3. When you hear yourself say something that is unreasonable or negative, immediately replace the statement with something reasonable and positive. Soon, you will be thinking of yourself fairly, in realistic and positive terms.

Summary

1. Make a statement about yourself.
2. Evaluate if negative (unreasonable) or positive (reasonable).
3. Replace negative with positive.
4. Record results and evaluate your progress

Recording Results

Using the following headings, make notations in your notebook.

Date	Quoted Statement + or -	Replacing (Positive) Statement
1/30	I can't get the notes right.	I can play as well as anyone.

Copy down every self-statement, no matter how unusual. You must rate the statement as either positive or negative. Replace all negative statements with positive ones; write these replacing statements down also. When you have entered all statements for a 15-minute session, draw a heavy line under the last entry to indicate when the session ended.

Evaluating Progress

Look at each "block" of statements closely. As you are seriously pursuing your goal, positive "Quoted Statements" will become more frequent than negative ones.

 **Negative statements and thoughts disappear as you work diligently toward your goal.**

Practicing Positive Self-Talk During Solo Physical Practice

Improve your execution through the influence of positive self statements. Force yourself to think — and act — positively when you practice until it becomes automatic.

1. Practice the physical skills, making sure that you are sitting or standing attentively and that you are executing correctly.
2. Then, play a passage or short exercise at least 60 times for positive self-talk practice. Before each attempt, make a positive statement to yourself right before you start to play. Make the same positive statement to yourself immediately after playing the passage or exercise.

Summary

1. Make positive statement about yourself.
2. Execute properly. Do not rush!
3. Repeat positive statement to yourself.
4. Record results in your notebook.
5. Evaluate your progress.

Recording Results

Although you do not have to write down the actual statement you made (you may, if you like), simply place a check mark somewhere on a page in your notebook to show that you made the positive statement before and after each attempt. You may allow a practice partner to record results and evaluate you. Simply make the positive statement before and after each attempt to your practice partner, and ask him or her to check off the attempt for you in your notebook.

Evaluating Progress

Look back at any notes you may have, paying attention to any indications that you may be performing better when you use the positive self-statements.

 Keep trying; it may take a few weeks of steady practice before you notice a significant change.

Practicing Self-Talk with Partner Intervention

Help yourself and your practice partner(s) eliminate all negative self-statements by replacing them with positive, reasonable statements.

1. Agree with your practice partner(s) to take a portion of practice (1 hour, for example) to evaluate your "thinking out loud" while playing.
2. While you are being evaluated, your partner should stop you whenever you say something negative and make you restate the item in a positive, constructive manner. Remember that positive words may be positive can be stated in a negative tone of voice, making the statement a hidden negative.
   - If you stop thinking out loud, your partner should prompt you by saying, "What are you thinking?"
   - If you respond with a negative statement, your partner should redirect you.
   - If your response is positive, then you are making progress on your own!
3. Be sure to reciprocate by switching roles and helping your partner at the end of your session.

Summary
1. Make statement about yourself.
2. Partner evaluates statement.
3. Partner redirects negative to positive.
4. Write down useful positive statements for reference.

Recording Results

Using the following headings, write in your notebook any positive statements that you feel comfortable with. Carry this list with you at all times for easy reference while you are building your new, positive habit.

Date	Situation	Positive Statement
4/16	Misread two measures	I'll correct it on the next time through.

Evaluating Progress

Whenever you have time, look at each statement closely. When practicing, always be aware of what you say to and about yourself.

 As you make progress, positive statements become second nature, with negative statements disappearing from your thoughts.

Changing Behavior During Sectional Practice

Help yourself and your playing partners eliminate negative behavior. **Assist each other in identifying negative behaviors and replacing them with positive behaviors.**

Your partners must agree 100% with the following game plan.

1. Any time a partner is observed acting in a negative, self-defeating manner, any other partner may stop and redirect him or her into positive behavior.
2. The redirected partner must identify what positive behavior would be more beneficial in a similar situation, write it down, and resolve to use the positive, replacement behavior the next time such a situation occurs.
3. **Optional:** To reinforce positive behavior and foster good spirit, have the offending partner contribute some money to the "kitty" each time a he or she is identified as saying or doing something that represents a negative self thought or behavior. Use the money at the end of the season to have a party or as a prize for the "most improved attitude."

Summary

1. Playing partners redirect each other during practice.
2. Offender identifies and writes down offending behavior, and resolves to use positive behavior.
3. Partners reinforce each others' positive behavior.

You Can Build Self-confidence!

Recording Results

Using the following headings, write in your notebook the positive, replacement behavior you will use the next time a similar situation occurs. Carry this list with you at all times for easy reference while you are building your new, positive habit.

Date	Situation	Positive Behavior
3/27	Started the attack carelessly.	I will concentrate on more decisive attack.

Evaluating Progress

Always before a performance and whenever else you have time, look at your notes on each situation and positive behavior closely. When practicing or in performance, always be aware of how you act.

 As you make progress, positive behaviors become second nature to you and your playing partners, with negative behaviors disappearing from your group's repertoire.

4 You Can Use the Super Powers of Your Mind!

When you accept the notion that whatever the mind believes, the body believes, you already have an enormous competitive edge. As you learn how to control what your mind believes, your ability to perform at maximum potential increases dramatically! The amazing thing is that you can use the power of your mind at home, at rehearsals, and on the job to improve the quality and consistency of your playing.

Visualizing Your Way to Success

The following sections describe the concept of visualization (mental practice or mental rehearsal). See **Mental Practice Drills** for detailed directions.

The Power of Mental Practice (Visualization)

Visualization is a classic example of focused imagination. Another name for it is mental imagery, or just imagery. If you imagine yourself practicing a skill, it is called mental practice. Every bit of it is as simple as ABC. Here is how it works with music.

To practice a particular passage, look at it closely; then just close your eyes and imagine that you are executing it perfectly. As a bonus, you can focus your imagination — just like a microscope — on any kind of situation you desire. If you are having trouble with air flow, imagine a well-supported, free flow of air through your instrument. If you are having trouble with a particular series of notes, set it up in your mind and "see" yourself executing the notes before you attempt to play them.

> **Example:** Mental practice is very effective and worthwhile. A research project conducted with basketball free-throw shooting provides the perfect example. Youngsters of equal ability were divided into three groups. Group 1 practiced free throws every day. Group 2 did nothing but use their imaginations to visualize perfect free-throw shooting every day. Group 3 did both.
>
> As you might guess, Group 3, the group that practiced both physically and mentally, did the best in the final test. But what surprises most people is that there were no significant differences between the group that only practiced physically and the group that only practiced mentally. Both groups significantly increased their free-throw shooting ability compared to their skill levels before testing. Visualized practice produced the same results in free-throw effectiveness as actual physical practice.

Obviously, real physical practice is necessary to develop the basic muscular skills. But this research demonstrates that correct visually-imagined practice does help to refine learned physical skills.

The best way to develop mental imagery skills quickly is to visualize both at home and in the practice room. As you develop the basics at home you will develop skill in visualizing the act of executing passages on the job.

Mental Practice at Home

You don't have to practice for hours on end to improve your playing. If you set aside at least 15 minutes for visualization, or success imaging, and practice faithfully, each day, for 8 days, you will see significant benefits in real situations.

Make a list of what you will practice. Sit in a comfortable chair in a quiet room and relax. Check off the instances on your list as your mental practice session progresses. You can visualize playing attacks, runs, phrases, melodic interpretations, etc., as well as coping with problem conditions and difficult situations.

The list of situations in which you can visualize success is as long as you desire. The idea is to always see yourself dealing with them successfully, in detail.

Performing Tough in Clutch and Disturbing Situations

When you know how to use mental practice, you can create clutch or otherwise disturbing playing situations in your mind and visualize yourself playing successfully during these situations — in other words, Performing Tough. Such elements may be noise, other people playing next to you, a high-stress performance, etc. First, you must identify specific high-pressure situations. Then, you can carry out the sequence, as shown, below.

Mental Practice for Performing Tough

Remember, your body believes what you tell it to believe. If you create a success history in your mind, that is what the body will react to, not the potential for failure. Your ability to perform up to your physical ability in real situations will increase!

 Tell your body that you can play successfully in both clutch and disturbing situations. It works! Take charge.

Combining Mental Practice with Physical Practice

You can put success imaging into real situations by combining mental practice with physical practice exactly as described below. By playing at least 60 practice passages each day for 8 consecutive days, you help to "lock in" the association between visualization of your execution of each passage. You will soon find that the visualization process takes an extremely small amount of time. In fact, regular playing partners may not even be aware of your new technique.

 Focus only on what is within your control — playing a high-quality passage.

Mental Practice During Performance

The success imaging process is useful right on the stage during a performance. Again, no one will know what you are doing. It's easy when you know how. As you wait for your turn, simply close your eyes for a few seconds and visualize an absolutely correct and complete passage, with excellent execution.

Your body takes this mental image of precision and success with it into your setup as you prepare to play. You must do this before every passage, no matter how easy or difficult!

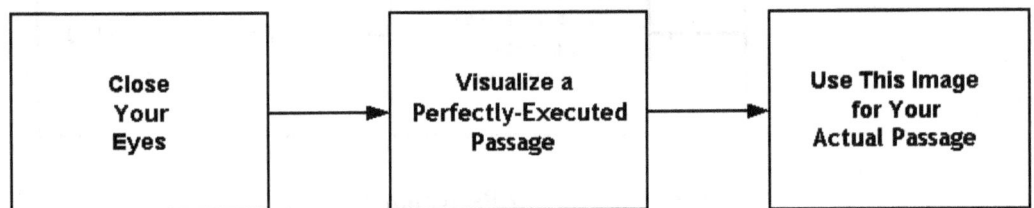

Mental Practice During Performance

In the chapter titled You Can Make Mental Toughness Routine!, you are given some additional preparation and organizing skills that make your consistent use of mental practice during a performance much easier.

 Visualizing success puts the odds in your favor, because you keep your mind focused on proper execution only and off of making mistakes or receiving recognition.

Visualizing with Video

Today, you can use video to see yourself instantly, anywhere — at home or in the practice room. You can help to refine and ingrain proper execution by watching a video recording of ideal technique.

When you are performing well, video record yourself and keep it for reference and review. It is helpful to watch yourself executing consistently well. If you are not executing well, you may watch a performance of someone else executing well. Do not watch someone who plays vastly different from yourself. For example, if you are a piano player with elegant movements, it could corrupt your form to watch a herky-jerky player with short, fast movements!

Watch the appropriate performance every day for 8 consecutive days, playing as soon as possible after each viewing. A variation of this technique is to take the video player to the practice room and watch yourself immediately before playing.

Endless Possibilities with Super Mind Power

As you can see, the power of your mind is awesome. Whatever your mind believes, your body will react to faithfully. You can have the competitive edge you desire by putting beneficial information into your mind. To do this, you must be selective.

Now you know how to use visualization to program your mind in practice or in performance. You can effectively visualize yourself executing correctly in all types of normal, clutch, and otherwise troublesome situations. You can be successful with mental imagery, all you must do is practice, practice, practice.

 **Everyone uses imaging. Those who imagine failure will probably fail. Those who imagine success will have a greater chance to succeed.**

Mental Practice Drills

For the drills on the following pages, keep a notebook so you can see your total progress. Label a page or section with the name of the drill at the top. Your notes are private, so keep them to yourself.

Mental Practice at Home or When Alone

Increase your ability to use mental practice (visualization) on a consistent basis to improve and maintain a high level of physical performance, by practicing at home. "Play" at least ten visualized passages per day. Never visualize missing your goal; there is no payoff for visualizing disaster except to create real disasters.

Directions

1. Draw up a chart in your notebook as shown under **Recording Results**.
2. Find a quiet place to relax and sit in a comfortable chair, but do not lie down during this drill because you need to make notes. You will check off the instances as your mental practice progresses.
3. Use the relaxation session to get yourself in a receptive state of mind before you start.
4. Visualize yourself doing the following drills for the elements of musical performance listed in **Table 1: Drills for the Elements of Musical Performance**, trying to make your visual image as real as possible; with all of the sights, sounds, smells, and other sensations normally associated with a real playing setting.

   Close your eyes and see and hear yourself setting up and executing each element perfectly. Take your time! Visualize your absolutely correct, perfectly executed element in detail. Do not visualize anything other than success.

Table 1: Drills for the Elements of Musical Performance

Element	Instructions for Visualization (See and hear yourself)
Tone	Playing long tones with a dark, full, warm quality of sound. This is affected by embouchure and air on a wind instrument.
Rhythm / Tempo	Playing while counting a beat and ensuring consistency.
Articulation / Precision	Playing all notes in tune from the attack to the end. This is affected by embouchure and air on a wind instrument.
Intonation	Playing short and long notes in tune. This is affected by embouchure and air on a wind instrument.
Balance	Playing a melodic passage, maintaining consistent attack and volume level.
Posture	Sitting upright and being attentive while executing any musical elements.
Phrasing	Phrasing passages expressively.
Style	Interpreting passages or entire compositions appropriately.
Dynamics	Playing passages using a wide range of volume while maintaining a good sound on every note.

Summary

1. Relax your mind and body.
2. Visualize success.
3. Record results.
4. Evaluate your progress daily.

Recording Results

Using the following headings in your notebook; make notes on the quality of your visualization for each and every element.

Date	Element	How Much Detail I Saw	How Thorough the Scene Was	How Crisp the Image Was
6/16	Phrasing	6	4	7

Evaluating Progress

Rate the characteristics above on a scale of 1 (worst or least) through 10 (best or most). Look for higher ratings over a period of 3 to 8 days.

Mental Practice for Clutch and Disturbing Situations (Performing Tough)

You can add specific negative elements to your mental environment and imagine yourself — in detail — playing music successfully under clutch and disturbing conditions. Use the following steps to identify real clutch and disturbing situations. You will use such situations while coping to reduce tension.

The situations presented in the table below are for illustration only; they may not be appropriate to your personal situation. They are fairly typical and are given to help you develop your own.

Table 2:   Typical Disturbing Situations

Associated with:	Type of Disturbance
Specators	Audible conversation while you are playing a quiet passage
	Excessive demand for your personal attention
	Yelling, coughing, or sneezing during the performance
	Past history of poor interaction with a specific individual
	Moving while in your line of sight
	Presence of a significant individual in a crowd
Other Musicians	Audible conversation in section while you are playing
	Having equipment clutter that impinges on your space
	Moving unnecessarily while in your line of sight
	Making unusual or inappropriate mannerisms
	Standing out of sight but making noise
	Making an inappropriate comment to you at any time
	Causing an unnecessary break in routine
	Past history of poor interaction with a specific individual
Internal	Lack of success in focusing thoughts
	Recent history of poor timing or technique
	Stiffness or tension not caused by a physical injury
	Inability to overcome challenges of the music in practice
	Inadequate preparation for intense performance
	Placing blame on previously trouble-free instrument
	Becoming excessively angry with a freak occurrence

Table 2: Typical Disturbing Situations

Associated with:	Type of Disturbance
Past Failures	Losing focus during a performance
	Losing concentration during the last few passages of a composition
	Making a mistake in transposition
	Misreading passages in similar situations

Summary for All Situations

1. Identify several high-pressure situations. Be specific.
2. Imagine yourself in the situation.
3. Visualize yourself executing calmly and perfectly.

Directions for Clutch Situations

1. In the spaces below, write a list of specific clutch playing situations that are real to you.

> **Example:** Typical clutch situations may be, "This piano is out of tune." "I cannot get my valves to stop sticking.", or "I get nervous when the player next to me taps his foot to his beat.", or "My reed has split, and I do not have another one." Think back to the conditions that produced high tension when you were in the clutch.

a. _____

b. _____

c. _____

d. _____

You Can Use the Super Powers of Your Mind!

e. _____

2. Now, visualize yourself in detail, playing in these situations. Focus only on perfect execution. Repeat visualization of a successful outcome at least 10 times a day for 8 consecutive days.

Directions for Disturbing Situations

1. In the space below, write a list of specific, disturbing playing situations. These should be real to you and affect you negatively in some way.

> **Example:** A typical situation may be, "I do not like to play with Joe, he disturbs my concentration." Another may be, "I do not play well in this hall." An off-stage example may be, "I do not like the people at the symphony's current location, they bother me."

a. _____

b. _____

c. _____

d. _____

e. _____

2. Now, visualize yourself in detail, playing in these situations. Focus only on perfect execution. Repeat your visualization of a successful outcome at least 10 times each day for 8 consecutive days.

Recording Results for All Situations

Draw up a chart in your notebook to record your observations. Using the following headings, make notes on the quality of your visualization for each instance.

Date	Element	How Much Detail I Saw	How Thorough the Scene Was	How Crisp the Image Was
7/11	Articulation	7	5	4

Evaluating Progress for All Situations

Rate the characteristic above on a scale of 1 (worst or least) through 10 (best or most). Look for higher ratings over a period of 3 to 8 days.

Mental Practice During Solo Physical Practice

You can put success imaging into real situations by combining mental practice (visualization) with physical practice. Then, you can make mental practice a part of your overall Mental Toughness Routine (MTR) in practice. See **Taking Control of Your Mental Environment**.

Directions

1. Draw up a chart in your notebook as shown under **Recording Results**.
1. Make sure that you are sitting up, maintaining good posture, attentive, and executing as correctly as you can.
2. **Then, play at least one passage for each element, visualizing a perfect result before each attempt,** as described in the exercise, **Mental Practice at Home or When Alone**, and summarized below.

Table 3: Visualizing and Playing Elements of Musical Performance

Element	Visualize First then Play the Following
Tone	Long tones with a dark, full, warm quality of sound. This is affected by embouchure and air on a wind instrument
Rhythm / Tempo	While counting a beat and ensuring consistency
Articulation / Precision	All notes in tune from the attack to the end. This is affected by embouchure and air on a wind instrument

Table 3: Visualizing and Playing Elements of Musical Performance

Element	Visualize First then Play the Following
Intonation	Short and long notes in tune. This is affected by embouchure and air on a wind instrument
Balance	A melodic passage, maintaining consistent attack and volume level
Phrasing	Passages phrsased expressively
Style	Passages or entire compositions interpreted appropriately
Dynamics	Passages using a wide range of volume while maintaining a good sound on every note

Summary

1. Relax your mind and body.
2. Visualize perfect setup, execution, and results.
3. Play a well-executed passage.
4. Record results.
5. Evaluate your progress daily.

Recording Results

Using the following headings in your notebook; making notes on the quality of your visualization for each and every element.

Date	Element	How Much Detail I Saw	How Thorough the Scene Was	How Crisp the Image Was
11/24	Style	7	7	6

Evaluating Progress

Rate the characteristic above on a scale of 1 (worst or least) through 10 (best or most). As the quality of your visualization increases, you will become more accurate and consistent. Look for improvement over a period of 3 to 8 days of serious application.

Mental Practice During Performance

Use mental practice (visualization) consistently before given passages during a performance to improve and maintain a high level of execution. Incorporate this habit of visualization into your Mental Toughness Routine (MTR) during performance.

Directions

1. Draw up a chart in your notebook as shown under **Recording Results**.
1. Make sure that you are sitting up, maintaining good posture, attentive, and executing as correctly as you can.
2. Then, if you have sufficient time, take about 3 to 5 seconds before you begin playing a passage to visualize, in detail, perfect execution of at least the first part of the passage. You may want to reserve visualization for only troublesome passages. Always picture yourself as being successful. **Refer to the section Combining Mental Practice with Physical Practice for instructions. The difference is that you will be visualizing all musical elements involved with what you are to perform.**

Summary

1. Relax your mind and body. Breathe appropriately for the task.
2. Visualize perfect setup, execution, and result.
3. Play a well-executed passage.
4. Analyze the passage and identify the element for improvement.

Recording Results

After you finish the performance, using the following headings in your notebook, write out which element needs correction and improvement.

Date	Element	Necessary Correction
4/14	Dynamics	More variety

Do not slow down the pace of performance for the other players; keep your recording activity short and to the point.

Evaluating Progress

As the quality of your visualization increases, you will become more accurate and consistent. Look for improvement over a period of 3 to 8 days of serious application.

5 You Can Relax, Anywhere, Anytime!

Believe it or not, relaxation is not "normal." Regardless of what people may think, they are almost never completely relaxed. Total relaxation while sitting in a chair may result in your sliding to the floor. Total relaxation while standing results in total collapse. Conversely, total tension results in not being able to move even your little finger.

To play your best during performance, you need the useful balance between relaxation and tension that you are accustomed to during your maximum-performance practice sessions. **Most players execute much better in practice because the stress of performance upsets the balance between relaxation and tension in favor of increased tension.** How can you make yourself execute better during performance? Let's think about two different ways. You could (1) practice under tense conditions or (2) perform under relaxed conditions.

Using Willful Relaxation

The following sections describe the concept of willful relaxation. See the "Relaxation Drills" section for detailed directions.

Practicing Under Tense Conditions

Practicing under tense conditions is not an efficient use of your time. Practice is the quiet time during which you can learn how to relax mentally and make repeated physical movements in a mentally-relaxed state. A quiet, low-stress atmosphere for practice allows your muscles to make fine, consistent movements — and to learn them.

Just think of those times when you tried to practice while someone near you was talking loudly or when you, yourself, were laughing and talking with friends! These types of disruptions create non-productive and often tense practice conditions. Practice under such conditions disturbs your concentration and does not allow your physical movements to be as refined — efficient or accurate — as when playing relaxed.

You Can Relax, Anywhere, Anytime!

Performing Under Relaxed Conditions

It is best to learn how to relax during performance. If it is possible to perfect your techniques under relaxed practice conditions, it only makes sense to mentally create the same conditions when you are in performance. You can learn how to make yourself relax during performance. As you develop this ability, you will discover that your relaxation-tension balance point is very close to what you experience during normal, noncompetitive practice situations.

Reaching Optimum Balance Between Relaxation and Tension

Few elements of nature work together with such consistency as the mind and body. Research tells us that, if the body's muscles are tense, then the mind is stressed. If the mind is stressed, then the muscles are tense. It is a vicious circle. Luckily for us, the opposite is also true. **If the body is relaxed, the mind is relaxed and clear.** If the mind is relaxed, the body is relaxed.

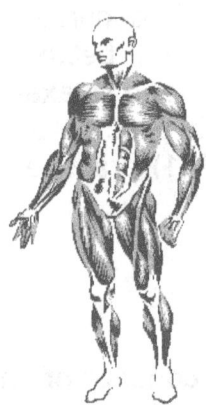

As you become more aware of bodily tension, you will discover that you have one particular muscle group (for example, jaw muscles, stomach muscles, forearm muscles, etc.) that tenses up before any other when you begin to react to stress. This sensitive muscle group, called a "threshold group", can serve as a trigger for your entire body. If it is tense, the rest of the body follows suit. However, when you can recognize the tension in that muscle group and relax it, the rest of the body will follow in a balanced manner.

Do not be concerned that you are learning to put yourself in an overly relaxed state. The natural tension that you feel when you really want to excel will not allow you to totally relax. The method you will learn in this book will not put you into a "deep" state of relaxation. It is designed to help you reach your own maximum balanced state between tension and relaxation that will allow you to execute at your peak physical level.

Recognizing and Relaxing Muscular Tension

The first step in learning to relax under stressful conditions is learning how to recognize muscular tension. The second step is learning how to replace excessive muscular tension with muscular relaxation. The key to achieving both lies in your mental awareness skills and your desire to change the state of your muscles.

To increase your awareness of the unbalanced muscular tension that places your ability to execute at risk, you have to first become aware of how tense you are under normal conditions. It is very difficult to recognize excessive muscular tension, because tension is a normal part of everyday life. Even many professional players never realize to what extent excessive muscular tension has eroded their ability to execute.

The most efficient way to learn how to recognize tension and to relax your muscles is by consciously alternating muscular tension and relaxation of the various muscle groups. At the end of the sessions, carried out exactly as described below, you will know clearly when you are under tension. You will be able to identify the primary muscle group and to actually relax those muscles when you want.

 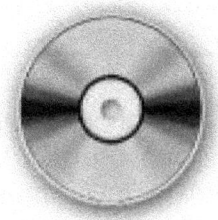

It really helps to listen to an audio relaxation session in which the speaker leads you in tensing and relaxing the various muscle groups.

> You may make your own relaxation tape or CD, following the directions given in Appendix B, "Making a Relaxation Tape or CD", or you can obtain a professionally-made version. Several general relaxation narrative sessions are available for purchase. Most of these contain a 20-minute activity that helps you learn how to recognize muscular tension and reduce it on demand.

Using the physical relaxation session, simply follow the directions in a quiet place where you can lie down and concentrate. After tensing each muscle group, always "let go" completely, returning to the beginning position and following the instructions to fully and completely relax that specific muscle group.

Participate by listening to the session 8 days in a row, each time trying to relax each muscle group more and more; taking it into an even deeper state of relaxation. Try to participate just before you practice and just before performance to acquire any real significant skill development in achieving muscular balance.

Using a Booster Tape or CD

It can be helpful to listen to a short-form, "booster" tape or CD of the relaxation session (about 5 to 10 minutes worth in your own voice) and a shortened coping session just before a major event. This booster is effective only after you have taken the regular eight-day program as explained above and are able to relax at will.

The objective is to focus only on your three most important (threshold) muscle groups that tense up the soonest or most often when presented with only the five most stress-producing situations with which you must cope. Think of it as an "express" way of calming down before performing.

See Appendix B Making a Relaxation Tape or CD for instructions on how to make your own, personal tape or CD.

 **Practice relaxation all of the time — at home, at work, and before and during every passage in practice and performance! Put relaxation practice to good use whenever you feel stress or muscular tension growing**

Relaxing in Real Playing Situations

We have developed an additional way to increase your skills even faster and with more specific confidence (don't forget the power of the mind). It involves your using another session after the end of your relaxation sessions **This is called a "coping session", because it assists you in coping with, or handling, difficult, real-life situations.** This session presents to you a set of example situations specific to your playing experience. You will add these, in your own voice, right on the tape or CD.

You can use the coping tape to extinguish your negative reactions to real and imagined clutch and disturbing situations that may have been causing anxiety and tension for a long time. You must use this coping strategy whenever you cannot calm yourself and play as relaxed as possible. Always use the coping strategy in anticipation of a performance and give yourself plenty of coping time beforehand.

> Note: The use of desensitization was studied (Norton GR, MacLean L, Wachna E: The use of cognitive desensitization and self-directed mastery training for treating stage fright. Cog Ther Res 2:61-64, 1978). A female pianist with chronic Musical Performance Anxiety, including memory lapses and tremors, successfully visualized herself actively coping with stressful performance situations. During a series of "practice performances" before small audiences, before and during which she deployed the coping strategies, she was able to prepare herself to execute successfully in an important competition and several concert performances. She reported that subjective anxiety, memory lapses, and tremulousness had all significantly diminished.

You must make this coping tape or CD session yourself; we cannot make it for you! Because you want to improve your ability to execute in real playing situations, the situations you pick to put on the tape or CD must reflect common playing situations for you. Thus, you can easily imagine that you are experiencing these situations because you actually have experienced them. **It is possible that you may not be aware of all things**

that bother you; therefore, it may be beneficial to identify these situations with the help of a sharp playing partner. For the coping session to be effective, these situations must be presented to you in a specific sequence.

Therefore, if you will follow the steps given below, you will maximize your potential to achieve a balanced performance under stress conditions. You may use our examples if they apply to you, buy you need to create specific ones for yourself. **Also, keep in mind that as you extinguish your negative reactions to a selection of clutch or disturbing situations, others may surface that you must extinguish. However, there will be a time when very little will disturb your concentration.** Look forward to that time!

See Appendix C Making a Coping and Booster Tape or CD for instructions on how to make your own, personal tape or CD.

Relaxation Drills

For these drills, keep a notebook so you can see your total progress. Label a page or section with the name of the drill at the top. Your notes are private, so keep them to yourself.

Practicing Willful Relaxation at Home

Be able to relax any muscle group on demand.

1. Draw up a chart in your notebook as shown under **Recording Results**.
1. Anytime you are lounging around at home, pick one muscle group to practice tensing and relaxing (see **Appendix B Making a Relaxation Tape or CD**).
2. Tense and relax that single muscle group 10 times in a row.
3. Repeat this drill with at least 3 different muscle groups daily for at least 8 days.

   To provide variety, have your spouse or a friend surprise you 3 times a day with a verbal request for you to relax a certain muscle group. For example, a friend may turn to you while you are watching television and say, "Left forearm — NOW!" You then have 5 seconds to completely relax your left forearm. With this type of assistance, your ability to relax spontaneously will improve over time.

Summary

1. Tense and relax 3 different muscle groups daily for at least 8 days.
2. Record your results.
3. Evaluate your progress daily after 3 days.

Optional: Relax on demand cue by spouse or friend.

Recording Results

Using the following headings, make entries in your notebook.

Date	Muscle Group	Relaxation Success
4/4	*Shoulder blades*	9

Evaluating Progress

Rate your "Relaxation Success", your ability to relax upon demand, on a scale of 1 (least) to 10 (most). After 3 days, look closely at your notes to see how well you are doing. Your ability to relax upon demand will increase significantly within 3 to 5 days and continue to improve with serious application. Each day, check to see what muscle groups need more work and focus on those during your next session.

Practicing Relaxation During Solo Physical Practice

Use this drill to increase your ability to relax and recover concentration and control during and after a distraction. **This drill makes you aware of your state of tension, as you see it.**

1. Draw up a chart in your notebook as shown under **Recording Results**.
1. Practice your instrument, making sure that you are sitting up properly, attentive, and executing correctly.
2. Play at least 60 short passages as well as you can.
3. **Distractions:** Ask your friends to interrupt your concentration at least 10 times without warning during this session. They may talk behind you, shout at you (do not disturb other players), walk up next to you while you are trying to concentrate, etc. However, they may not touch you or bring harm to anyone.

Summary

1. Execute 60 short passages as well as you can.
2. Relax and recover your concentration quickly when disturbed.
3. Record results.
4. Evaluate your progress.

You Can Relax, Anywhere, Anytime!

Recording Results

Using the following headings, make entries in your notebook.

Date	Passage #	Type of Distraction	Execution Quality	Ability to Relax	Ability to Concentrate
10/6	16	Noise	6	4	2

Evaluating Progress

Rate your "Execution Quality", "Ability to Relax" and "Ability to Concentrate" on a scale of 1 (poorest) to 10 (best). After 3 days, look closely at your notes to see how well you are able to relax and recover under stress.

Practicing Relaxation During Supervised Physical Practice

Use this drill to increase your ability to relax and recover concentration and control during and after a distraction. **This drill makes you aware of your state of tension, as your observer sees it.**

1. Draw up a chart in your notebook as shown under **Recording Results**.
1. To improve your ability to relax after a distraction, practice while being watched by an observer. Make sure that you are sitting up, maintaining good posture, attentive, and executing as correctly as you can.
2. Then, play at least 60 short passages while being watched by an observer.
3. **Distractions:** Ask your friends to interrupt your concentration at least 10 times without warning during this session. They may talk behind you, shout at you (do not disturb other players), walk up next to you while you are trying to concentrate, etc. However, they may not touch you or bring harm to anyone.

Summary

1. Execute 60 passages as well as you can.
2. Relax and recover your concentration quickly when disturbed.
3. Have your observer record results.
4. Have your observer evaluate your progress.

Recording Results

Using the indicated headings in your notebook, do the following:

1. Write down your own passage-by-passage evaluation of your "cone of focus" (how well you seem to be relaxing and concentrating); **always include what you think you are doing while you are attempting to recover from distractions.**

2. Have your observer write down an evaluation of what he or she observes about your relaxing and concentration, i.e. **what you are visibly doing while you are attempting to recover from distractions.**

Signs the observer should look for include: (ability to relax) your grinding your jaw, squeezing a towel, jiggling your leg, tapping your fingers, etc.; (ability to concentrate) your looking around at the score or watching other players, talking unnecessarily, etc.

Date	Passage #	Type of Distraction	Execution Quality	Ability to Relax	Ability to Concentrate
8/7	43	*Someone called my name.*	8	5	7

Evaluating Progress

Have your observer record the "Type of Distraction", then have him or her rate "Execution Quality", "Ability to Relax" and "Ability to Concentrate" on a scale of 1 (poorest) to 10 (best). After 3 days, look closely at your notes to see how your evaluation compares with that of your observer. **You may be quite surprised to discover what another person sees!**

Using Willful Relaxation During Performance

Develop the ability to relax on demand, increasing your concentration and control during a real or staged performance. Until the skill of willful relaxation is "locked in", you will have to monitor yourself and make notes. **Do not slow down the pace of performance for the other players; do your recording activity after the performance, short and to the point.**

1. Draw up a chart in your notebook as shown under **Recording Results**.
1. First, make sure that you are sitting up, maintaining good posture, attentive, and executing as correctly as you can.

2. During performance, as you are waiting to play, evaluate the quality of your relaxation and concentration. Try to correct any errors made during a previous passage on your very next similar passage — do not wait!

3. As soon as you have time, write down an honest evaluation of how well you played a passage in question. Do not allow yourself to be influenced by the outcome; uptight people sometimes play acceptably well, and relaxed, focused people occasionally make mistakes.

Summary

1. Relax your mind and body.
2. Play a well-executed passage. Do not rush!
3. Analyze and evaluate execution, relaxation, and concentration.
4. Write down your evaluation.

Recording Results

Using the following headings, make notes on your behavior in your notebook.

Date	Passage #	Execution Quality	Specific Error/ Correction	Ability to Relax	Ability to Concentrate
11/1	21	9	*Insufficient air flow*	7	6

Evaluating Progress

Rate your "Execution Quality", "Ability to Relax" and "Ability to Concentrate" on a scale of 1 (poorest) to 10 (best). If you made an error, write it down under "Specific Error/ Correction", along with your strategy for correcting it — e.g. "...missed accidental after quarter rest — did not transpose measures...." Review your notes after each competitive session (as time allows).

6 You Can Make Mental Toughness Routine!

All players unconsciously develop patterns of thinking that they use as they set up to play. Many develop thinking habits that are not very productive. They usually arise from a non-conscious level but, regardless of their source, they do not foster superior performance.

For consistently good performance, you must consciously establish a set of productive thinking habits that allow you to execute at your peak performance potential every time.

To get you on your way, we encourage you to try our Mental Toughness Routine, or MTR. It combines the mental skills we have shown you so far into an easily-learned sequence that you use before playing. It is a proven approach to establishing a strong pattern of productive thinking. If you use this routine consistently, clutch situations will have minimal impact on your ability to perform. You will truly be Performing Tough!

Taking Control of Your Mental Environment

The MTR helps you stay on task during performance. But, you must maintain control of your thoughts and actions at other times as well. To provide a good mental environment for the MTR to work effectively, do the following.

- **Prepare your mind before you arrive at the engagement.** Use your relaxation tape or CD, mental practice, and positive self-statements as a way of focusing your mind on what you are about to do.

  "Psyching up" is actually calming down while being alert to the task. Maintain this focused attitude for the entire time you are "on the job." You may abandon this attitude after the performance ends.

- **Be sure to have used your coping tape or CD to extinguish any negative reaction to disturbing thoughts and situations.** It is extremely important to start out with a clean emotional slate! Let nothing cause you anxiety; take charge.

- **During the performance, talk only if absolutely necessary to maintain the progress of the music.** This is not a way of "psyching out" others! In fact, it has nothing to do with others. It is simply a way to keep your mind in the skills. For example, you may break your concentration to confer about something on the score, but once the issue is resolved, resume concentrating on your skills.

- **Do not visualize anyone else playing while you are trying to program your mind for performance!** To do so will corrupt the image you have of yourself playing. The only image you want in your mind is your own successful performance.

- **Between passages, keep others from talking to you unnecessarily by avoiding prolonged eye contact.** If you have to speak about something important, do so; but do not engage in a long conversation.

Mental Toughness Routine

The Mental Toughness Routine (MTR) is an organized series of activities that you use to increase the quality and consistency of your execution.

The MTR helps you control only that over which you have direct control — execution. More consistently successful performances will follow.

The MTR works by keeping your mind focused on beneficial thoughts and actions while you are performing. At the same time, it keeps thoughts of failure out of your mind. As you get into the habit of using the MTR, it becomes much easier to use. It will not be automatic, however, so you must use it consciously all of the time — especially during performances.

Take a quick look at the Mental Toughness Routine Flowchart on the following page, paying special attention to the boxes, their headings, and the beneficial activities under each heading.

Each box represents a phase, or period of time. One phase flows into the next. Beneficial activities occur during each phase and are, themselves, arranged into rough time slots. Beneficial activities may be mental or physical. Let's look a little closer at what happens during each phase.

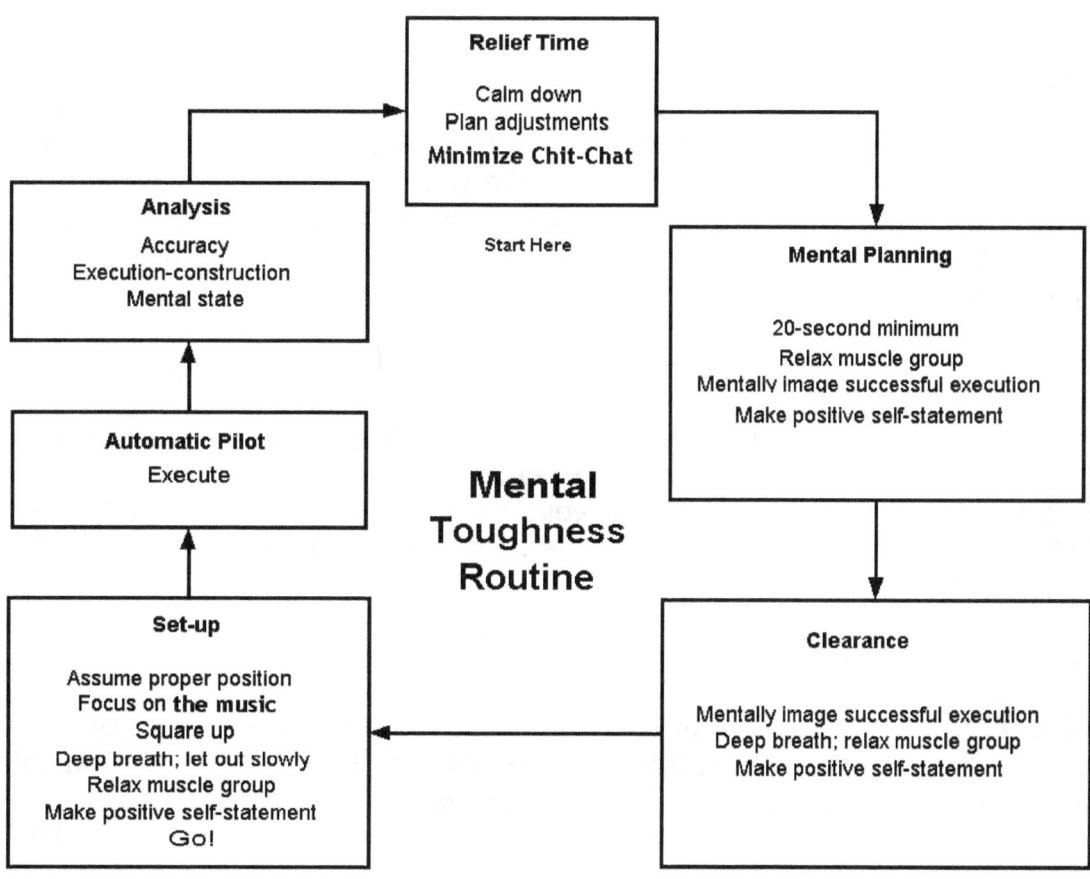

Relief Time

Relief Time begins just after your previous passage. It lasts until you play again. After completing a passage, be calm and plan for the next passage. Although you do not need to begin focusing your attention on execution during this stage, it is still important to talk only when absolutely necessary. Remain calm and focused.

Mental Planning

Mental Planning begins after Relief Time. It is the time during which you begin a concentrated effort to focus your thoughts and apply your mental skills. As you learned earlier, you probably have a threshold muscle group that tenses up first when you are under pressure. Relax this muscle group. Then, imagine yourself successfully executing. Make a positive statement to yourself. Keep repeating your mental imagery and positive self-statements until it is your turn to play again. Be aware of muscle tension and relax as needed.

Clearance

Clearance compares to the "batter up" period in baseball. It is the time when you are preparing to set up for playing. Don't rush, take your time! Imagine yourself playing a passage successfully, either from memory or while reading the music. Given time, repeat this until the passage is clear in your mind. When finished, set up. Take a deep breath and make a positive self-statement.

Setup

Setup is the preparation period just before you play. Make sure that you are sitting up, maintaining good posture, attentive, and executing as correctly as you can. Do not cut your setup time short. Focus your eyes on your music and take a deep breath. Relax your threshold muscle group. Make a positive statement to yourself. When your mind is quiet, you can begin to play.

Automatic Pilot

Automatic Pilot means that you play without being overly conscious of your movements. To do this with confidence, you must be well-practiced. Your physical movements should be so ingrained that your execution is reliable every time.

Analysis

Analysis is the time immediately following your passage. During this time, you must realize what was correct or incorrect with your execution. You may not have "felt" right. Your mental state may not have been the best. At any rate, take time to analyze your previous passage. Also, do not start any conversation until <u>after</u> you have completed your analysis.

MTR Incorporation Drill

Use this drill during practice or during a staged performance to help you incorporate all of the habits you have learned from previous chapters into your Mental Toughness Routine (MTR) during performance.

During practice, carry a copy of the MTR in your pocket so you can refer to it quickly during your Relief and Mental Planning phases. Until a skill is "locked in", you will have to monitor your development in all competitive situations. **Do not make notes until after the performance; do not slow down the pace of performance for the other players; keep your analysis and note-taking activity short and to the point.**

> When you are certain that you use all of the mental techniques consistently, you will not have to make notes. However, if you experience lapses in concentration and in correcting errors, run this drill again, until you are performing effectively.

1. As you are walking to your chair, evaluate the quality of your relaxation, concentration, and execution.
2. Make sure that you are sitting up, maintaining good posture, attentive, and executing as correctly as you can.
3. After you finish a passage, make an honest evaluation of it. Do not allow yourself to be influenced by the outcome; uptight people sometimes play well, and relaxed, focused people do occasionally have off times!
4. Plan and resolve the correction of any errors on your very next similar passage – do not wait!
5. Run all of the the MTR steps that precede your next passage, including relaxation, visualization of perfect execution, and positive self-talk.

Summary

1. Relax your mind and body.
2. Play a well-executed passage.
3. Analyze and evaluate relaxation and concentration.
4. Write down your evaluation if possible.
5. Plan and resolve how to correct errors.
6. Run MTR.

Recording Results

Using the following headings, make notes on your performance in your notebook.

Date	Passage #	Ability to Relax	Ability to Visualize	Positive Self-talk	Ability to Analyze	Ability to Correct
12/12	17	7	9	6	4	5

Evaluating Progress

Rate the effectiveness of your "Ability to Relax", "Ability to Visualize", "Positive Self-talk", "Ability to Analyze", and "Ability to Correct" on a scale of 1 (poorest) to 10 (best). If you made an error, write it down in the "Ability to Correct" column, after your numerical rating. Review your notes after each performance (as time allows).

As you incorporate the techniques into your MTR, your actions will become automatic, your execution will improve in all situations.

A Final Word

Good playing is playing your best and improving your playing during the next passage! Smart playing involves correcting all of the time — keeping your head in the skills. Performing Tough is smart playing under pressure!

To Perform Tough effectively all of the time, do the following consistently.

1. **Practice your physical skills to know how your body should feel during an excellently-played passage.**

    No matter what your error, do not be critical of yourself — only constructive. Your objective is to think positively and productively so you can correct any errors in the very next instance.

2. **Collect your beneficial thoughts and actions into an organized Mental Toughness Routine and use this routine all of the time.**

3. **Stay focused on the only goal that is under your control — executing all of the musical elements of a passage successfully.**

Performing Tough is a privilege available to anyone. After finishing this book you now know enough to be as tough a player as your physical ability will allow you to be. Best of luck for future success!

You can Perform Tough! Put what you have learned into practice every day and Perform Tough with the best!

You Can Make Mental Toughness Routine!

Appendix A Building Reliable Physical Skills

This section includes a list of instructional books to help you refine your musical capabilities. Over the years, music has had wonderful teachers and performers that have attempted to share with readers what has been successful for them. Fortunately, unlike some other disciplines, music instructors usually agree on a uniform set of techniques that have been successful for others. Therefore, the majority of modern players approach music in a similar fashion.

These books may make similar recommendations, but the authors may state their cases in different language. Also, some authors may have prioritized their recommendations in a different order. **However, regardless of the insight to be gained from these books, it is vital that you work with a good instructor to structure a reliable playing technique. Then you will be able to apply the mental skills more effectively.**

Popular Music Performance Books

As recommended by GoodReads online (https://www.goodreads.com/shelf/show/music-performance; top rating = 5)

Ludwig van Beethoven: Complete Piano Sonatas, Volume 1 (Nos. 1-15) by Ludwig van Beethoven (shelved 2 times as music-performance) Ratting 4.52 — 166 ratings — published 1935

Suzuki Violin School, Vol 5: Violin Part by Shinichi Suzuki Ratting 3.95 — 33 ratings — published

Suzuki Violin School, Vol 4: Violin Part by Shinichi Suzuki Ratting 4.23 — 46 ratings — published

The Structures and Movement of Breathing: A Primer for Choirs and Choruses/G5265 by Barbara Conable Ratting 4.35 — 29 ratings — published 2000

The Musician's Way: A Guide to Practice, Performance, and Wellness by Gerald Klickstein Ratting 4.30 — 623 ratings — published 2009

The Great Pianists by Harold C. Schonberg Ratting 4.33 — 730 ratings — published 1963

Great Contemporary Pianists Speak for Themselves by Elyse Mach Ratting 4.42 — 60 ratings — published 1991

Great Pianists on Piano Playing: Godowsky, Hofmann, Lhevinne, Paderewski and 24 Other Legendary Performers by James Francis Cooke Ratting 4.20 — 77 ratings — published 1917

Molto Agitato: The Mayhem Behind the Music at the Metropolitan Opera by Johanna Fiedler Ratting 3.59 — 128 ratings — published 2003

The King and I: The Uncensored Tale of Luciano Pavarotti's Rise to Fame by His Manager, Friend and Sometime Adversary (Hardcover) by Herbert Breslin Ratting 3.52 — 84 ratings — published 2004

The Inner Voice: The Making of a Singer (Hardcover) by Renée Fleming Ratting 4.13 — 981 ratings — published 2004

The Perfect Rehearsal: Shawnee Press Vocal Library by Timothy Seelig Ratting 4.25 — 10 ratings — published 2006

Pitch Perfect: The Quest for Collegiate A Cappella Glory (Hardcover) by Mickey Rapkin Ratting 3.40 — 4,129 ratings — published 2008

Suzuki Violin School, Vol 6: General MIDI Disk CD-ROM (Audio CD) by Linda Perry Ratting 4.00 — 7 ratings — published 2002

Fiddling Handbook [With CD] by Craig Duncan Ratting 2.00 — 1 rating — published 1997

A Guide to Non-Jazz Improvisation: Fiddle Edition [With CD] by Dick Weissman Ratting 4.00 — 2 ratings — published 2007

Best of Cole Porter by Hal Leonard Publishing Company Ratting 4.33 — 12 ratings — published 1992

The Harold Arlen Songbook by Harold Arlen Ratting 4.88 — 15 ratings — published 1985

How to Write Songs on Keyboards - A Complete Course to Help You Write Better Songs Book/CD (Softcover) by Rikky Rooksby Ratting 4.00 — 62 ratings — published 2005

Thesaurus of Scales and Melodic Patterns (Hardcover) by Nicolas Slonimsky Ratting 4.50 — 88 ratings — published 2012

Effortless Mastery by Kenny Werner Ratting 4.13 — 1,747 ratings — published 1996

Lexicon of Musical Invective: Critical Assaults on Composers Since Beethoven's Time by Nicolas Slonimsky Ratting 4.33 — 222 ratings — published 1953

The Life and Death of Classical Music by Norman Lebrecht Ratting 3.59 — 157 ratings — published 2007

The Harmony of Bill Evans by Jack Reilly Ratting 4.00 — 18 ratings — published 1994

The Harmony of Bill Evans, Volume 2 [With CD (Audio)] by Jack Reilly Ratting 5.00 — 7 ratings — published 2010

The Bill Evans Trio - Volume 1 (1959-1961): Featuring Transcriptions of Bill Evans (Piano), Scott Lafaro (Bass) and Paul Motian (Drums) by Bill Evans (Contributor) Ratting 4.75 — 9 ratings — published 2003

The Bill Evans Trio - Volume 2 (1962-1965): Artist Transcriptions (Piano * Bass * Drums) by Bill Evans (Contributor) Ratting 0.0 — 2 ratings — published 2003

The Bill Evans Trio - Volume 3 (1968-1974): Artist Transcriptions (Piano * Bass * Drums) by Bill Evans Ratting 0.0 — 2 ratings — published 2003

Symmetrical Scales For Jazz Improvisation by Masaya Yamaguchi Ratting 3.50 — 7 ratings — published

The Songwriting Sourcebook by Rikky Rooksby Ratting 3.98 — 110 ratings — published 2003

Songwriters Playground: Innovative Exercises in Creative Songwriting by Barbara L. Jordan Ratting 3.64 — 41 ratings — published 1993

19 Sonatas - Complete: Piano Solo by Wolfgang Amadeus Mozart Ratting 5.00 — 13 ratings — published 1986

Etudes: Piano Solo by Frédéric Chopin Ratting 4.60 — 33 ratings — published 1985

Complete Preludes, Nocturnes and Waltzes: For Piano by Frédéric Chopin (Composer) Ratting 4.67 — 101 ratings — published 2006

The School of Velocity, Op. 299 (Complete): Piano Technique by Carl Czerny (Composer) Ratting 4.12 — 50 ratings — published 1969

Complete Bach Transcriptions for Solo Piano by Franz Liszt Ratting 5.00 — 5 ratings — published 2003

Kind of Blue by Miles Davis Ratting 4.10 — 44 ratings — published 2000

A Love Supreme: The Story of John Coltrane's Signature Album by Ashley Kahn Ratting 4.22 — 1,251 ratings — published 2002

The Billy Joel Keyboard Book: Note-For-Note Keyboard Transcriptions by Hal Leonard Publishing Company (Creator) Ratting 4.55 — 37 ratings — published 1993

Early Advanced Classics to Moderns: Music for Millions Series by Denes Agay Ratting 4.11 — 17 ratings — published 1969

Piano Music of Béla Bartók, Series II by Béla Bartók Ratting 5.00 — 5 ratings — published 1982

Bela Bartok: An Analysis of His Music by Erno Lendvai Ratting 4.56 — 70 ratings — published 1971

Craft of Musical Composition: Book One, Theoretical Part (Tap/159) by Paul Hindemith Ratting 4.17 — 154 ratings — published 1942

The Craft of Musical Composition, Book 2: Exercises in Two-Part Writing by Paul Hindemith (Composer) Ratting 4.47 — 82 ratings — published 1976

Norton Anthology of Western Music by J. Peter Burkholder (Editor) Ratting 4.05 — 53 ratings — published 2009

Norton Anthology of Western Music, Volume 1: Ancient to Baroque by Claude V. Palisca Ratting 4.16 — 135 ratings — published 1980

Hearing and Writing Music: Professional Training for Today's Musician by Ron Gorow Ratting 4.22 — 279 ratings — published 1999

Learn to Read Music by Howard Shanet Ratting 3.50 — 139 ratings — published 1964

Appendix B Making a Relaxation Tape or CD

> Note: As an authorized purchaser of Playing Tough, you may download Dr. J. C. McCroskey's Relaxation audio in MP3 format from http://www.roberthstrickland.com/Relaxation/Relaxation.htm. (Case Sensitive) Click "Download the relaxation audio here." When prompted, type the User Name: "purchaser" and the Password: "authorized."

If you would like to make your own complete relaxation session or the shorter, more focused, booster session(s) on tape or CD, here are the instructions.

Making a Relaxation Tape or CD

The physical relaxation session focuses on all of your muscles and several of your most stressful situations. On direction of the narrator (in this case, yourself) you are given the opportunity to learn how to tense and relax your muscles completely at will, in a quiet place where you can lie down and concentrate. We recommend that you listen to the relaxation session two times per use.

1. Get a tape recorder and a blank audio cassette tape with at least 30 minutes of recording time on a side. The reason is that you need to record two identical relaxation sessions on one side and leave ten minutes blank so you can record a coping session right after it, as described in Chapter 5. Alternatively, you can record directly onto a computer or digital recorder and copy the .wav or .mp3 file to a CD.
2. Find yourself a nice, quiet place to record.
3. Record the following introduction on only the first part of your tape or CD. Speak slowly.

    "Close your eyes, lie on your back and relax (the "beginning position"). Place your arms at your sides with the palms down. Look inward to sense the satisfying feelings of true relaxation. Let your muscles go and search for the deep, deep pleasure of full relaxation.

(Pause for a while to give yourself time to reach full relaxation!)

Now, we are going to start a series of actions that involve alternating the tension and relaxation of specific muscle groups throughout your body. As you tense a muscle group do not try to produce extreme levels of tension; you may pull a muscle! Good solid tension will do the job — just enough so you can tell, without a doubt, that the muscle group is tense."

4. Record the following instructions for each muscle group (body part), using a higher, sharper tone of voice when you want to reflect tension and a lower, softer tone of voice when you want to reflect relaxation.

> Note: We use the muscle group of the left and right hands to illustrate the pattern for recording. When you are actually recording, substitute the muscle group and its accompanying tension instruction in the proper places indicated by parentheses, below.

"Start with your (left hand). (Make a fist) and increase the pressure. Hold it ... now, relax. Feel the muscles relaxing and the pleasant feelings as the muscles fall deeper and deeper into complete relaxation.

(Leave enough time to tense and relax and to feel complete relaxation!)

Try it again. Tense your (left hand), feel the muscles getting tense and rigid. Hold it ... now slowly relax the muscles. Feel the (left hand) getting loose and the muscles becoming free and lying back against the bones.

(Leave enough time to tense and relax and to feel complete relaxation!)

Now try your (right hand) . (Make a fist) and increase the pressure. Hold it ... hold it ... now relax. Feel the muscles relaxing and the pleasant feelings as the muscles fall deeper and deeper into complete relaxation.

(Leave enough time to tense and relax and to feel complete relaxation!)

Try it again. Tense your (right fist), feel the muscles getting tense and rigid. Hold it .... now slowly relax the muscles. Feel the (right hand) getting loose and the muscles becoming free and lying back against the bones."

Continue, following the instructions, below.

Muscle Group	Tension Instructions
Left Hand	"Make a fist."
Right Hand	"Make a fist."
Back of Lt. Hand	"Tilt your hand backward at your wrist."
Back of Rt. Hand	"Tilt your hand backward at your wrist."
Left Biceps	"Press your left fist against your left shoulder."
Right Biceps	"Press your right fist against your right shoulder."
Left Foot	"Curl your left toes toward your heel, tighten your foot."
Right Foot	"Curl your right toes toward your heel, tighten your foot."
Left Calf	"Point your left toes away from your knee, tense your calf."
Right Calf	"Point your right toes away from your knee, tense your calf."
Left Shin	"Bend your left foot upward toward your knee; make it tight."
Right Shin	"Bend your right foot upward toward your knee; make it tight."
Left Thigh	"Straighten your left leg; make your thigh muscles hard."
Right Thigh	"Straighten your right leg; make your thigh muscles hard."
Stomach	"Make your stomach hard, like a brick."
Chest	"Tense up your chest muscles, make them hard."
Shoulders	"Bring both your shoulders up to touch your ears."
Front of Neck	"Lift your head and press your chin into your chest."
Back of Neck	"Push your head back, press against the surface."
Tongue	"Press your tongue up against your roof of your mouth."
Eyes	"Squeeze your eyes shut and lower your eyebrows."
Forehead	"Wrinkle up your forehead."

5. Re-record the relaxation session once: It should take about 10 minutes to record the session, so go ahead and record it again on the second 10-minute portion of the tape or CD. This will make your two relaxation sessions about 20 minutes long.

6. **Listen to the sessions. After tensing each muscle group, always "let go" completely, returning to the beginning position and following the instructions to fully and completely relax that specific muscle group.** Give yourself sufficient time to return to the beginning position and to feel the complete relaxation; you will need approximately 10 seconds of quiet time.

7. Repeat the listening session 8 days in a row. Each time, try to relax each muscle group more and more, taking it into an even deeper state of relaxation.

Appendix C Making a Coping and Booster Tape or CD

If you will follow the steps given below in making your own, personal coping tape or CD, you will maximize your potential to achieve a balanced performance under actual stress conditions. You may use our examples (see **Table 2, Typical Disturbing Situations**, page 56) if they apply to you, or you may create special ones for yourself with peoples' specific names.

Making a Coping Tape or CD

1. Identify three **low-stress playing situations** that do not cause you any undue stress or muscular tension. Put these situations into an "experiencing" sentence. Remember, these situations do not cause you stress; they are either pleasurable or neutral.

   > **Example:** "I am practicing with my best friend.", or "I am showing my young niece how to play.", or "I am just playing for fun, improvising on my instrument."

   Write out your **low-stress playing situations** below. Place the most pleasurable one first and the neutral or least pleasurable one last.

   a. _____
      _____
      _____

   b. _____
      _____
      _____

c.
_____
_____
_____

2. Now, identify any three **moderate-stress playing situations** that cause you a small to moderate level of stress or muscular tension. Using the same format, list these situations in the spaces below.

> **Example:** "I am getting ready to warm up as the other players are arriving.", or "The first three members of my section are laughing and talking near my as I am playing exercises.", or "I'm playing in a concert and everyone is waiting to hear me solo.", or "I am in a performance and have lost my place in the music."

Remember to use situations that work for you. If you're a professional player, the situations that cause you moderate stress are different from those that cause moderate stress for a recreational player.

Write out your **moderate stress situations**. Place the least tension-producing one first and the most tension-producing one last.

d.
_____
_____
_____

e.
_____
_____
_____

f.
_____
_____
_____

3. Finally, identify three **high-stress playing situations** in which you experience high levels of stress or muscular tension. Use the same method as above.

> **Example:** "I have vigorously launched in to a solo, but have already made a couple of mistakes.", or "I missed a key change four measures earlier in the score.", or "One of my section mates is out of tune, and he does not realize it.", or "I broke a string on my cello, and the end of the composition is still 32 measures away."

Remember, these should be troublesome situations to you. The experiences should really "bother" you.

Write out your **high stress situations** below. Place the least tension-producing one first and the most tension-producing one last.

g. _____

h. _____

i. _____

4. Wind your relaxation tape forward to the end of the relaxation session or record into a computer and add the .wav or .mp3 file after the relaxation session on the CD. Record in your own voice the following introductory instructions at the start of the coping session.

    "I am going to imagine myself in a series of playing situations. As I mentally imagine the situation to be real, I will make every effort to recognize tension and relax the muscles in my body. When I recognize muscular tension, I will focus on that specific muscle group and enjoy relaxing it."

5. Then, record the situation statements you listed in a "low, moderate, high" sequence. Use a convincing voice and record them in the specific order shown below. Make a statement every 30 seconds; let there be complete silence until you make the next statement (that is, a 5-second statement, followed by approximately 25 seconds of silence). **This silent time is when you willfully relax your muscles in response to the situation!**

    A-B-C - B-C-D - C-D-E - D-E-F - E-F-G - F-G-H - G-H-I

    Statement A (low) is first, followed by statement B (moderate), then by statement C (high). Then drop statement A and repeat statements B and C, adding statement D (low). Then drop statement B and repeat statements C and D, adding statement E (moderate). Repeat this pattern until you have recorded all of your statements.

    Be sure to leave silence after each situation statement.

6. In the peace and quiet of your home, select a place where you can lie down (bed, sofa, recliner, etc.) and where you will not be interrupted by anyone.

7. Turn on the sessions at a comfortable volume, listen to the relaxation and coping sessions, doing exactly what you are told to do. Imagine yourself in each real coping situation. **Stay awake! If you fall asleep, you will have to start the session all over again!**

    Each time you hear a coping statement, pay attention to how your body reacts to it. Focus on relaxing any muscles that become tense as a reaction to the statement. Deliberately and consciously relax the reactive muscle group or groups during the silence that follows each statement.

8. **Listen to the relaxation and coping sessions each day for 8 consecutive days. At the end of that time, you will be able to recognize tension and reduce it whenever you want and in response to real situations. You will consciously relax under pressure! You will be in control!**

Making a Booster (Relaxation with Coping) Tape or CD

The "booster" tape or CD is a short-form version of the full relaxation session; it runs for only about 5 to 10 minutes, in your own voice. A shortened coping session is placed after the relaxation session (see *Appendix B Making a Relaxation Tape or CD*). Use it just before a major event. This booster is effective only after you have taken the regular eight-day program as explained above and are able to relax at will. It focuses on only your three most important (threshold) muscle groups and five most stress-producing situations.

Directions

1. **Relaxation Session**: Follow the same pattern as the long version described above. However, do not record the introduction, and record a session that deals with only your three threshold muscle groups. Record it only once.

2. **Coping Session**: Add a session dealing with only the five situation statements you listed that give you the greatest amount of stress. Make a statement every 30 seconds, leaving approximately 25 seconds of silence after each statement to feel and reduce tension. Because there are only five statements made three-at-a-time, the specific order is:

    E-F-G - F-G-H - G-H-I - H-I

    Listen to the situation statements. Pay close attention to see which muscles react by becoming tense. Then, deliberately and consciously relax the reactive muscle group or groups during the silence that follows each statement.

Index

A

analysis 76
anger
   productivity 18
anxiety
   nervousness 20
   obstacle to smooth execution 21
   part of performance 26
anxious 26
audiotape
   relaxation 65
automatic pilot 76

B

behavior
   changing with practice partner 45
   negative 38
booster CD 66

C

CD
   booster 66
   relaxation 65
clutch situation
   examples 16
   how it develops 13, 15
   impact on performance 20
   personal 16
   pressure 13
   professional players 14
   stress 13
coping 67
   CD 89
   tape 89
correcting
   smart playing 78

D

decisions
   conscious 34
   non-conscious 25
drills
   mental practice 54
   relaxation 68
   self-talk 44

E

emotions
   negative 18
   out of control 18
execution
   mechanically poor 33
   mental practice drill 55, 59
   tips for reliability 81

F

failure
   belief that you will fail 29
   event production 38
   fearing 27
   potential 14
focus
   detraction by behavior 38
   mental toughness routine 74
frustration
   factors beyond your control 39, 40, 41
   release by behavior 39

G

goal
   unreasonable 17

H

help
   jointly, by playing partners 41
herky-jerky player 53

I

instructor
   ongoing relationship 22

K
keyed up 31

M
mattering
   non-belief 30
mental planning 75
mental practice
   at home 51, 54
   drills for improvement 54
   during performance 52, 61
   during physical practice 59
   on the stage 52
mental toughness routine
   focus 74
   MTR 73
mind power 53
movements
   trusting 22
MTR
   mental toughness routine 73
   phases 74
muscle tension
   recognizing 65
   stress 64

N
negatives
   effects of thought 14
   eliminating 40
   recognizing 39, 42, 43
   replacing with positives 40, 43

O
odds
   knowing 27
on-stage situation
   visualization 58

P
partner-assisted behavior changing 45
performance
   impact of clutch situations 20
   mental practice 52, 61
   relaxation during 68
performance system
   incorporating behaviors 34
Performing Tough 13
phases of MTR 74
playing situations
   high-stress 90
   low-stress 89
   moderate-stress 90
playing smart
   correcting 78
practice
   mental skills 33
   partner-recorded results 45
   physical game only 33
   tense conditions 63
programming
   talking to your brain 37

R
relaxation
   attaining a deeper state 88
   audiotape 65
   balance with tension 63
   CD 65
   drills for improvement 68
   during performance 68
   during solo practice 68
   not normal 63
   practice at home 68
   real situations 67
relief time 75

S
self-talk
   at home 44
   drills for improvement 44
   partner intervention 45
setting up clearance 76
setup 76
skilled player

vs tough player 97

stress
   clutch situation 13
   high level and performance 18
   immunity 26
   muscle tension 64
   overcoming with mental skills 27
   overpowering 31
   part of performance 26
   performance 63, 68, 89
   personal 16
   recovery from 70
   relaxing 65

stressed-out 26

success
   fearing 28

T

talking to others
   effects 38

teacher
   ongoing relationship 22

tensing up
   trying harder 31

tension
   balance with relaxation 63

thinking
   positive 37
   productive 73

threshold muscle groups 66, 92

tough player
   vs skilled player 97

trying harder
   tensing up 31

V

video
   visualization 53

visualization
   mental practice 49
   on-stage situation 58
   video 53

Performing Tough is successfully meeting the mental challenge of performing well, regardless of the difficulty of the music or the amount of pressure. The difference between a skilled player and a tough performer is that the tough performer applies the appropriate mental toughness skills consistently! This is a privilege available to anyone.

After finishing this book you will know enough to be as tough a performer as your physical ability allows. If you seriously and consistently apply the lessons described, you will incorporate the behaviors into your performance system that make sense to you, that fit your personality, and allow you to reach your goals.

You can:

Build Self-confidence!

- Increase your confidence through what you say to yourself and others.
- Establish the correct frame of mind for success.
- Act like a success.

Use the Super Powers of Your Mind!

- Visualize successful performance.
- Practice anytime, anywhere.
- Focus your mind for consistent, successful performance.

Relax, Anywhere, Anytime!

- Relax physically and mentally.
- Set and achieve realistic goals for yourself.
- Increase your knowledge of yourself and how you really feel about and react to real situations.

Make Mental Toughness Routine!

- Organize your thoughts and actions for consistent, high-level performance in practice and in performance.
- Apply useful knowledge and practice, practice, practice!

Will Powers, Ph.D., is retired Professor Emeritus of Communication Studies at Texas Christian University in Fort Worth, Texas. He has published over 150 books, articles and papers while conducting clinics and training programs around the world. Together with his wife, Lois, he has established a highly-successful management and career development consulting business showcasing the Tip-A-Day concept, a daily approach to developing enhanced communication skills. The current product is called Concept Keys.

For the past 18 years, Will has been helping people in the workforce perform at quality levels while under pressure (including executives, managers, speakers and athletes of all types). This book is an effort to bring those years of experience and specialized knowledge to the music industry on a national level.

Bob Strickland, M.S. was raised in Dallas, Texas; his mother was a violinist who taught him an appreciation of classical and jazz music. His earliest memories of music are from age three, when he first heard his mother's 78 RPM records of Tommy Dorsey, Stan Kenton, Woody Herman, Harry James, and Gene Krupa. Developing a keen interest in the music and the musicians, he eventually became a jazz and big band historian, familiar with hundreds of different musicians, arrangers, and styles. Bob has been playing trumpet since the age of 22, studying with Joe P. Cinquemani of the Dallas, Fort Worth, and Houston Symphonies, and with Clint McLaughlin, himself a student of Don Jacoby.

Bob began leading his own performing groups in 1973, and from 1994, until moving to Everett, Washington in 2002, he led and performed with his 17-piece big band, Swingtime 2000. In 1967, he was awarded an NDEA Title IV fellowship to pursue graduate study in science and education at the University of Georgia. Having studied biomechanics and kinesiology at TWU in Denton, Texas, Bob continues to apply his scientific knowledge and educational training to music and other technical disciplines in his own, unique way. He and his wife, Sue, own and operate Robert H Strickland Associates LLC in Everett, Washington, helping businesses improve operations through strategic planning and documentation.

www.ingramcontent.com/pod-product-compliance
Lightning Source LLC
Chambersburg PA
CBHW080347170426
43194CB00014B/2717